W9-AXR-488

PENGUIN BOOKS

The Mafia Handbook

Douglas Le Vien, Jr., a.k.a. Tomasso Russo, is now executive assistant to the Brooklyn District Attorney. A street-smart New York City Police detective raised in South Brooklyn, he infiltrated the Sicilian and American Mafia in New York City. After a stint in the federal witness protection program, he served publicly from 1984 to 1986 on the President's Commission on Organized Crime. He is a nationally recognized expert on the mob.

Juliet Papa is an award-winning reporter for 1010 WINS Radio in New York City. Her assignments have included the world of organized crime and some of the city's most sensational trials. She was born, raised, and still lives in New York.

To my wife, Barbara, and my two sons,
Douglas III and Vincent, for their eternal
patience and understanding
— D. Le V.

To my family,
the only one that really counts
— J.P.

The Mafia

HANDBOOK

Everything You Always Wanted to Know about the Mob But Were *Really* Afraid to Ask

Douglas Le Vien, Jr. and Juliet Papa

WITH ILLUSTRATIONS BY ED MURAWINSKI

Penguin Books

PENGUIN BOOKS
Published by the Penguin Group
Penguin Books USA Inc., 375 Hudson Street,
New York, New York 10014, U.S.A.
Penguin Books Ltd, 27 Wrights Lane,
London W8 5TZ, England
Penguin Books Australia Ltd, Ringwood,
Victoria, Australia
Penguin Books Canada Ltd, 10 Alcorn Avenue,
Toronto, Ontario, Canada M4V 3B2
Penguin Books (N.Z.) Ltd, 182–190 Wairau Road,
Auckland 10, New Zealand

Penguin Books Ltd, Registered Offices: Har-
mondsworth, Middlesex, England

First published in Penguin Books 1993

1 3 5 7 9 10 8 6 4 2

Copyright © Douglas Le Vien and Juliet Papa, 1993
Illustrations copyright © Viking Penguin,
a division of Penguin Books USA Inc., 1993
All rights reserved

Concept by Doris O'Donnell and Doug Le Vien

LIBRARY OF CONGRESS CATALOGING IN PUBLICATION DATA
Le Vien, Douglas.
The Mafia handbook: everything you always
wanted to know about the mob but were *really*
afraid to ask/Douglas Le Vien, Jr., and Juliet
Papa; with illustrations by Ed Murawinski.
p. cm.
ISBN 0 14 01.7589 X
1. Mafia—United States—Humor. I. Papa, Juliet.
II. Title.
HV6446.L4 1993
364.1'06'0973—dc20 92-43591

Printed in the United States of America
Set in Transitional 521,
a digitalized version of Electra
Designed by Tony Libido
Illustrations by Edward Murawinski

Many of the characters in *The Mafia Handbook* are caricatures designed for comic effect. The Mafia does not and should not define an entire ethnic group. It is our hope that any negative stereotypes will one day go the way of cement shoes.

—D. Le V. and J.P.

Acknowledgments

Thanks to "Joe" Hynes, Brooklyn District Attorney, Kings County, for his inspiration and motivation; Ken McCabe, Criminal Investigator, U.S. Department of Justice, Southern District of New York—the best of the best; and all others whose names have been withheld to protect their safety.

— D. Le V.

There are many people whose expertise, guidance, and common sense made this book happen. Special thanks go to WINS Radio anchor Eileen Douglas and WINS reporter Carol D'Auria; to WINS News Director Steve Holt and Executive Editor Steve Swenson; to WINS General Manager Warren Mauer, who said to me after I covered John Gotti's 1992 trial, "You should write a book about this stuff"; to Joe

Carella, John Bracco, Patricia Hurtado, Diane Beni, Fran Saporito, all true friends; to law enforcement officials who prefer anonymity; to Jerry Schmetterer for sharing past experience; to agent Julian Bach; and to editor Dawn Drzal for her wicked wit.

I am truly thankful to my attorney, Bob Stein, for his invaluable advice and support.

My thanks to the wiseguys—for better or for worse.

I cannot express enough appreciation to my parents and my brother for their unconditional love.

And finally, to Douglas A. Le Vien, Jr.: Who's got it better than you?

— J.P.

Contents

Chapter One

The Deformative Years

The Deformative Years

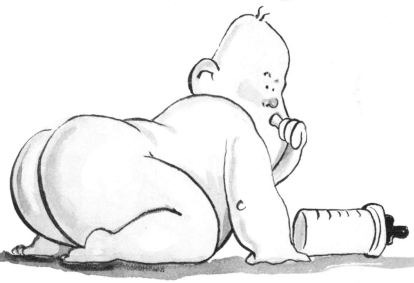

Sweet Mystery of Life

Okay, so you're wondering how that perfect baby boy, that darling bundle in the lace christening gown straight from Sacred Heart Church, grows up to be called "Sammy the Bull." It's a journey of enlightenment toward "made man" that begins at birth and doesn't end until the fat lady sings. Or he does (or gets "whacked," whichever comes first).

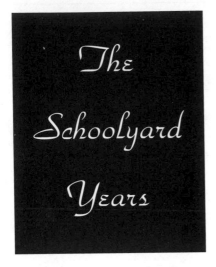

The

Schoolyard

Years

Barely out of his First Holy Communion suit, the nascent toughguy becomes immersed in what amounts to Introduction to Organized Crime 101, a crash course in street shenanigans. Do you think anyone learns these techniques in Sister Honorata's eighth-grade social-studies class? Any trainee worth his bullets knows he's got to start somewhere. So he explores:

Trunking:

Screwdriver, please. Pick a block full of parked cars. The eager trainee quickly becomes adept at popping those rear locks and making a quick and easy getaway with whatever he can grab from the trunk. As he gathers speed and expertise, the toughguy trainee will be able to scan the contents in an instant and scoop up what he knows will sell on the street, thus earning him brownie points with his idols and mentors, the wiseguys back at the social club. Once they see that the new kid continues to bring in those golf clubs, suitcases, and tool chests, they'll regard him as a possible recruit.

Fireworks:

A quick bang for the buck in a seasonal market. But to maximize profits, the trainee quickly learns the art of the "double bang." That means he tells his supplier that the police took his batch and he needs another. In fact, he's already sold the original load and has pocketed the money for himself before going back for more. The astute trainee knows he can pull off this stunt just so many times before he ends up on the wrong end of an M–80.

Gambling:

Armed only with a deck of cards, a pair of dice, and a wad of cash, the opportunistic trainee can round up a game anytime, anywhere from the candy store to the confessional. This entry-level position, when performed with diligence, competence, and the proper tools (marked cards, loaded dice), offers the promise of rapid advancement to the more lucrative and personally fulfilling field of loan-sharking.

Junior Bookmaking:

Where the "action" is. The art of this steal is the trainee's ability to finesse young friends or neighborhood old-timers into trusting him with their bets. The more business he brings to the local bookie, the more the trainee profits, since he collects a percentage of the action. Consistent growth helps build a solid reputation in underworld finance.

Growing Up Wiseguy

SALVATORE GRAVANO
"Sammy Bull"
Underboss (1990-91)
Consigliere (1988-90)

"Nature or Nurture: One man's testimony on criminality, personal accountability, and environmental causality" by Salvatore *"Sammy the Bull"* Gravano, **Ra.T.**

GRAVANO: When you grow in a neighborhood like I grew in, and you grew with the people I grew with, it was an environment. I was a kid.

ALBERT KRIEGER *(defense lawyer):* Go ahead.

GRAVANO: When I was a kid I was involved in gangs, dropped out of school in the eighth grade. It was an environment. It was not something . . . I just grew with it. It didn't seem wrong, the whole life-style didn't seem wrong.

KRIEGER: In effect, the devil made you do it?

Gravano: The devil didn't make me do it. I did it on my own.

KRIEGER: Okay.

GRAVANO: But the life-style did.

KRIEGER: I guess that what you are saying is that you want . . . you want the world to think of Sammy Gravano as a poor victim of environment and circumstances, correct?

GRAVANO: I don't want the world to think anything.

A Criminal Psychologist Responds

Sammy the Bull's environmental impact statement didn't impress the experts. Dr. Gerald Lynch, criminal psychologist and president of the John Jay College of Criminal Justice in New York, comments:

There are many different criminal subcultures, and the Mafia is one of them. And in that group, there are a separate set of expectations. It's not uncommon for members to cleverly retreat into the "it's not my fault, but the culture I grew up in" argument. But it's hard to believe that someone would use it, unless they are slightly retarded, or don't have their wits about them. In the Mafia, the life of crime is a way to prove virility and manhood, to gain acceptance. Part of that is achieved by distorting right from wrong. The explanation smacks a lot of trying to wriggle out of it, by saying "I didn't know what I was doing when I was robbing, cheating, and stealing."

Evolution of a Wiseguy:

Make new friends, increase your earning power in 7 easy steps.

You gotta be *looked at:* Is he mob material? The wannabe is given the "once-over" to make sure he has what it takes. That means, among other things, taking orders, taking heat, taking money from Cousin Louie's business, if he has to.

You gotta be *schooled:* Trained in the Ways of the Wiseguy. The fine art of picking up a piece, carrying numbers, driving the getaway car.

You gotta be *groomed:* He learns the appropriate swagger and sneer. He buys his first hand-tailored suit and a pair of see-through socks. Once he starts looking and acting like one, the wannabe is well on the road to becoming the real thing.

You gotta *make your bones:* The wannabe is now entrusted with a big job, usually a "hit," to test his courage and to see whether or not he'll throw up at the sight of all that blood.

You gotta be *vouched for:* The wannabe's mob mentor does the right thing when he thinks his protégé is ready—which he'd better be, because the wannabe knows the consequences if he lets his sponsor down.

You gotta be *proposed:* It's time to check the credentials. This process includes making sure the wannabe hasn't double-crossed somebody along the way. It also means checking to see who his grandmother is. Cross-references are necessary, so his name is passed along to other Families for their review.

You're *MADE!:* It's time to slip on the suit and tie and meet the Don; the solemn ceremony is bigger to him than his wedding day, but the vows are just a bit different.

Nouvelle Cugine

After he drops out—or, more commonly, gets thrown out—of school, the young wannabe is free to pursue full-time his goal of being noticed. The first step, of course, is to look the part. The wannabe, known familiarly as the *cugine* (pronounced koo-jheen'), always dresses to expose the most flesh possible. Tank tops are a must because they reveal his powerful biceps— necessary for strong-arming or breaking a kneecap or two. It's common practice for the wannabe, even if he's an Extra Large, to buy all his shirts in size Small. The tightest possible jeans ensure that he'll

The Cugine

walk with the requisite swagger. At the other extreme is the loose-fitting pair of Champion sweatpants, sometimes cut-off, with open-laced, high-top Nike sneakers. They provide the appearance of athleticism and enable the cugine to flee from danger when no one's looking.

His car is an important extension of himself. No self-respecting wannabe is properly equipped without the mandatory black IROC Camaro. If there isn't a twenty-five-pound *cornu* (horn) hanging from the rearview mirror (to ward off the "evil eye"—of the cops—and to bring good luck—with the babes), it's a big red bow with dangling ribbons that obstructs about 85 percent of the windshield. The cugine usually drives by peering through the loops.

Now that he's achieved the look, the cugine has to get the girl, commonly referred to as the "cugette" (pronounced koo-jhet'). In doing so, he's paving the way for acquiring one of the finer accoutrements of mob life—the mandatory mistress, or "goumada." (The actual spelling of the word is "comare," which means, literally, "godmother." For purposes of pronunciation, however, we'll render the word as "goumada" throughout the book.) The cugine will always keep his eye on Maria, the neighborhood "good girl" from St. Joseph's Convent School, because that's whom he'll eventually marry (she always liked bad boys, anyway) But for now, gum-chewing, smart-mouthed Antoinette will do just fine. She looks great at parties, at weddings, next to the cugine in the car; she's the perfect accessory (or alibi?). Her clothes must be as revealing as his, although for different reasons. She is easily identifiable by her one defining characteristic:

BIG HAIR!

The Cugette

Cugine Mating Call

Cugette on sidewalk outside pizzeria, leaning on car with friends. Cugine pulls up in black GT with tinted windows. Goes inside, passes group of cugettes, eyes the lot, meets with Tony, Nicky, and Vito about the line on Sunday's football game. Returns to car and singles out a girl:

CUGINE: Hey—
CUGETTE: Yeah?
CUGINE: You.
CUGETTE: Whatchya lookin' at? Take a picture. It lasts longer. (*Cugettes all laugh and chew gum at the same time.*)
CUGINE: C'mere.
CUGETTE: (*Saunters over to car.*)
CUGINE: Wanna go?
CUGETTE: 'kay. When?
CUGINE: Now.
CUGETTE: I got my period.
CUGINE: FUGGEDABOUDIT!!! (*Peels out and speeds off!*)

Climbing the Ladder in Heels
(cugette wardrobe)

Gum

60 pairs of earrings (hoops with inter-changeable balls and charms)

10 gold chains

1 diamond-encrusted gold name necklace

1 diamond-encrusted first-initial ring

1 Fossil watch

1 gold I.D. bracelet

1 gold ankle bracelet with engraved initials

9 pairs of Versani heels in assorted colors plus 6 pairs of black

12 pairs of spandex pants in assorted colors plus 6 pairs of black

20 midriff-exposing tops in assorted colors, 8 in white with various rhinestones/sparkles/sequins/studs

6 pairs of Jordache/Guess jeans in various stages of fading

1 black leather motorcycle jacket acrylic nails/tips—jewel encrusted, stripes, decals. Manicurist popular in neighborhood for inventing her own designs.

Hair to THERE

Ten steps to truly enormous hair:

1. Apply half a jar of mayonnaise to hair; cover head with plastic wrap, then tin foil.
2. Shampoo, using *Brolage Hair Salon Formula with Extra Body*.
3. Slather on *Brolage Extra Rich Conditioner*; rinse.
4. Blow-dry with round brush.
5. Use curling iron sparingly.
6. Drench with *Image* mousse.
7. Scrunch.
8. Apply *Matrix* gel liberally.
9. Hang head over bed, tease with pick to give lift.
10. Spray liberally ("Ozone? Oh, yeah, Ozone Park. My sister lives there.") with *Sebastian* aerosol hair lacquer.

The hours spent achieving hair that looks like a wig is time well spent, according to the cugette. That's because it means her hair will NEVER fly out of control when the cugine puts the top down or opens the sunroof. It means she'll still look great after a long night of making out. And it means her hair will retain its composure, even when she doesn't, which is often.

The cugette's vast knowledge of haircare

also makes her a fine candidate for Angelina's Beauty School. Her experience with many varied salon products gives her a leg up on the competition in this grueling academic pursuit. She can probably even skip Basic Styling and advance to the more demanding upper-level course, How to Cover the Roots. Graduation from Angelina's may soon be followed by elevation to the exalted status of goumada, or Mafia mistress, as the beauty parlor has traditionally been a favorite mob front, and where better to meet that young cugine on the rise than in a back-room bookmaking or loansharking operation? She'll already know how to manage the place, and she'll probably be her own best customer.

Dollars and Scents

The cugette will spare no expense in looking—and smelling—good. She wants to make sure she leaves a lasting impression wherever she goes and on whomever she's with. Not one to leave anything to chance, the cugette first lays the groundwork with an array of aromas—starting with "passion fruit"–flavored lipstick, "fresh-scent" deodorant, and baby powder. But after the basics, the cugette lets out all stops with powerful designer fragrances. Topping the list are *Escape* by Calvin Klein, *Opium* by Yves St. Laurent, *Trésor* by Lancome, and *Amarége* by Givenchy. Body lotions are a must, especially if they don't match the brand-name perfumes.

This veritable riot of scents is guaranteed to send the cugine reeling, not because he's falling madly in love but because he's suffering from an allergic reaction.

The Name Game

During his rite of passage, the wannabe will no doubt earn himself a nickname. Sometimes it stems from an activity or personal habit he acquired as a kid. For example, Patty "Boxcars" was good at dice. Joey "Pipes" smoked one all the time. Sometimes the name can be an unkind reference to the way he looks. Consider "Big Pete" Chiodo, weighing in at almost 500 pounds, and Vinny "The Chin" Gigante.

Their so-called chosen "profession" can also play a role in getting a name that sticks. Billy "The Butcher" Maselli had his hooks in the meat business, and Joe Profaci was known as "Mr. Olive Oil" because of his import empire.

In other cases, the nickname is bestowed as a badge of honor. Anthony Corallo, for example, was called "Tony Ducks" not because he harbored a fondness for small, fluffy, web-footed creatures but because of his uncanny ability to avoid prison. Carmine Lombardozzi was called "The Doctor" because, as master loan shark, he "took care" of people's

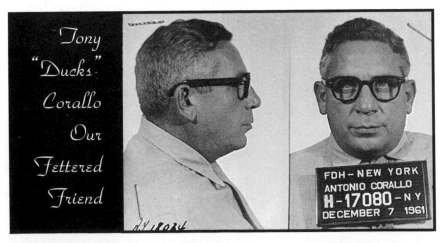

Tony "Ducks" Corallo Our Fettered Friend

FDH – NEW YORK
ANTONIO CORALLO
H-17080 – N Y
DECEMBER 7 1961

money problems. As for "Sammy the Bull," it was once commonly held that the short, stocky amateur boxer was named for his demeanor in the ring. Only later, when the Bull turned rat, did his former friends and colleagues readily offer the revisionist spin: The Bull is, and always was, full of it.

Nicknames also come in very handy if you have to tell the difference between family members who have the same name. For instance, Carmine Persico's brother is Alphonse. He's known as "Alley Boy." Carmine's son is also Alphonse, but the family had the creative inspiration to call him "Little Al." John Gotti's son is also John; he's called "Junior." But of course, there's always the exception to the rule. Take Vic Orena, "Little Vic," whose son Vic Orena is also called "Little Vic."

Vinnie "The Chin" Gigante sporting his daytime ensemble of pajamas, bathrobe, and matching cap, in custody for mob dress-code violation

Nicknames

Albert "The Mad Hatter" Anastasia
Anthony "Tough Tony" Anastasio

Tommy
Flounderhead

Joseph "Joe Piney" Armone
Joe "Bananas" Bonanno
Vincent "The Fish" Cafaro
Anthony "Gas/Gaspipe" Casso
Paul "Big Paulie/The Pope" Castellano
Anthony "Tony Ducks" Corallo
Joseph "Joe Butch" Corrao
John "Jackie Nose" D'Amico
Alphonse "The Professor" D'Arco
James "Jimmy Brown" Failla

Carmine "Charley Wagons" Fatico
Arthur "Dutch Schultz" Flegenheimer
Jimmy "The Weasel" Fratianno
Christopher "Christy Tic" Furnari

Joey Apples

Carmine "Lillo/The Cigar" Galante
Joseph "Crazy Joe" Gallo
Albert "Kid Blast" Gallo
Lawrence "Kid Twist" Gallo
Sam "Momo" Giancana
Vincent "Vinny the Chin" Gigante
John "Good-looking Jack/Jack the Actor" Giordano
Salvatore "Sammy the Bull" Gravano
John "Junior" Gotti Jr.
Matthew "Matty the Horse" Ianniello

Joseph "Socks" Lanza
Philip "Crazy Phil" Leonetti
Salvatore "Sally Dogs" Lombardi
Thomas "Three Fingers Brown" Lucchese

Harry Cigars

Charles "Lucky" Luciano
Venero "Benny Eggs" Mangano
Carmine "The Snake" Persico
Thomas "Tommy Karate" Pitera
Salvatore "Jersey Sal" Profaci
Angelo "Quack Quack" Ruggiero
Andrew "Mush" Russo
Salvatore "Tom Mix" Santoro
Benjamin "Bugsy" Siegel
Carmine "Mr. Gribbs" Tramunti

Looking for Trouble

Although the wiseguys may not seem to be paying him any attention, the cugine is under as much scrutiny as any IBM trainee. There are certain litmus tests that determine whether he's management material.

Situation #1

A senior member of the *brugad,* or Family, says to the wannabe: "Here's a grand in small bills. Make sure it's right and take it to Sal at Ennio's." In fact, he will have handed the wannabe more than $1,000, perhaps $1,100.

What should the wannabe do? (The answer may be self-evident to *you.*)

a. Pocket the extra hundred dollars and buy the gold *cornu* he's had his eye on.

b. Return the extra hundred with a small smile and tell the capo politely that he must have miscounted.

c. Forget to count the money at all because he bumps into Joey Big Ears on the way.

The answer, of course, is "b." If the wannabe gets a reputation for "going south," or stealing from his own colleagues at this stage, it will be all but impossible for him to redeem himself.

Situation #2

A capo tells the cugine to stand look-out in front of the bakery in which a mini-casino occupies the back room. If the cops arrive, he's instructed to yell inside, "Hey Joey, I need coffee." The cugine should:

a. Tell his girlfriend to bring the car around, so they can park in front of the bakery and make out.

b. Yell inside the bakery, "Hey Joey, I need a cannoli," just as a goof.

c. Remain outside, focusing intently on all passersby for any sign of trouble.

The answer is "c." Even the most humorless of wiseguys enjoys a good goof every now and then, but there's a time and a place for everything. Since this surveillance scenario does not qualify as such, the cugine is well-advised to exercise self-restraint.

Situation #3

The capo instructs the cugine to break the plate-glass window of Tony's Candy Store, since Tony is late in repaying the loan shark. The cugine will:

   a. Step away from the mirror and go break Tony's window.

   b. Take his cugette to see *Tony and Tina's Wedding* and break the window tomorrow.

   c. Break the window and take twelve cartons of cigarettes from inside.

The answer is "a." If he answered "b," the cugine probably won't be going to the theater or anywhere else for quite a while. When the capo wants something done, it's done on *his* timetable. Answering "c" is incorrect because the cugine would be overstepping his bounds by stealing the cigarettes. Tony shouldn't have to suffer twice—not yet, anyway.

Southwest Brooklyn "In" spots

The ambitious cugine will come to learn that southwest Brooklyn is the place to see and, more important, be seen by the wiseguys he hopes to impress. Bensonhurst, Bath Beach, and Gravesend are fertile ground for wannabes. All roads lead to the main thoroughfares: 86th Street, 18th Avenue, and Bath Avenue—"Mob Midways," where a dizzying array of restaurants, cafés, bars, and funeral parlors serve the discriminating wiseguy as popular meeting places, and resting places.

Restaurants

Tommaso's
1464 86th St.

Milano's
7514 18th Ave.

Ponte Vecchio
8810 4th Ave.

Rossini's
8712 4th Ave.

Villa Vivolo
8829 26th Ave.

Mille Luce's
7123 18th Ave.

Social Clubs

Veterans and
Friends
1446 86th St.

Veterans and
Friends
1628 Bath Ave.

Pompeii
6705 11th Ave.

Italia
6921 18th Ave.

West End Club
1714 Bath Ave.

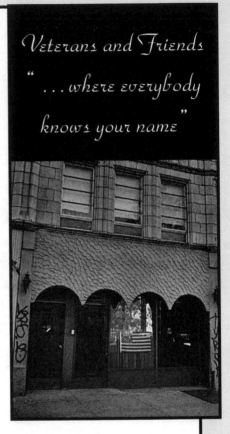

Veterans and Friends

" ...where everybody knows your name "

Bars/Lounges

Secrets
6201 11th Ave.

Cropsey Lounge
1861 Cropsey Ave.

The Rex Manor
1100 60th St.

Funeral Homes

Scarpaci's
1401 86th St.

Cusimano and Russo
2005 W. 6th St.

Torregrossa
345 Avenue U

La Bella
2625 Harway Ave.

Scarpaci hearse: It's curtains

Nebraska Diner

Diners

Vegas Diner
1619 86th St.

Nebraska Diner
2939 Cropsey Ave.

Carroll Gardens

Just a few miles north of the hub of activity, Carroll Gardens has a Family life all its own:

Restaurants

Monte's Venetian Room
451 Carroll St.

Marco Polo
345 Court St.

Casa Rosa
384 Court St.

Nino's
215 Union St.

Social Clubs

Nestor Club
Between 235 and 237, on 5th Ave.

451 Club
451 Court St.

Par 3 Golf Club
453 Court St.

Carolyn's
461 Court St.

Funeral Homes

Cusimano and Russo
230 Court St.

Raccuglia
323 Court St.

The *restaurant* is a good starting point for the cugine. He'll hang around, but, more important, schlep around. When he's not running errands for his superiors, he should at least drop some serious money as a show of respect. Wiseguys are always in restaurants for two very good reasons: 1) because they're great places to conduct "business" and 2) because eating is one of their favorite pastimes. If they see the cugine around often enough, they'll know he's earnest and he's trying. The cugine should make sure, however, that he doesn't become a pest.

The *social club* remains the center of the mob universe, where made members, seeking a refuge from the anxieties of the workaday mob world, indulge their fondness for overeating, card playing, and stringing together obscenities. While they're leisurely sipping espresso, or waiting for the cook to finish whipping up the chicken cacciatore, the cugine can rustle up a few odd jobs, run more errands, or bring in his score from a successful night of trunking. If he's good, the cugine will manage to get somebody's attention. Maybe it'll be the Boss, who comes for his weekly meetings every Wednesday night. Those social club schedules are good to know. Even though the wiseguys are always there to hang out, there are certain times for "business hours":

Social Club Business Hours

Bergin Hunt and Fish Club
98–04 101 Ave., Queens
Saturday, 2–4 p.m.

Veterans and Friends
1446 86th St., Brooklyn
Sunday, 11 a.m.–2 p.m.

Veterans and Friends
1628 Bath Ave., Brooklyn
Monday–Friday, 1–4 p.m.

West End Club
1714 Bath Ave., Brooklyn
Sunday, 10 a.m.–12 noon

Rayfield Club
17th Ave., Brooklyn
Sunday, 11 a.m.–2 p.m.

Hawaiian Moonlighters Club
140 Mulberry St., Manhattan
Wednesday, 7–9 p.m.

Pizzerias are an early training ground for the routine of the social club. Here the cugine gets an early start on selling football sheets, playing cards, taking bets, and eating. With enough practice, he'll dish out and collect money as fast as Vinny whips up a pie "to go."

Bars and lounges, those dark, smoke-filled rooms with the tacky decor, serve important functions. They are, in effect, the mob's post offices. Information is exchanged subtly and expeditiously. If the cugine makes a habit of stopping by for a drink (the bar is usually stocked with liquor from the latest hijacking), he'll begin to pick up the cues; he'll start recognizing the significance of the casual hand-off of a nondescript envelope or brown paper bag; and he'll understand the urgency of conversations concerning shipments for "twenty cans of olive oil" from Sicily or "fifty pounds of coffee" from South America.

The wannabe's favorite hangout may be the twenty-four-hour diner because it affords round-the-clock opportunity to watch the wiseguys in action. Diners are a good place for business transactions because mobsters can easily switch tables if they don't like the guys sitting next to them. They're also conveniently located right off the exits of major highways—easy to get to, or get away from, as the case may be. Best of all, any seat offers an unobscured view of vehicular traffic into and out of the parking lot. It is here that the cugine is instilled with a healthy sense of foreboding at the sight of a silver El Dorado with Florida plates.

Because attending wakes is one of the wiseguy's most important activities, the wannabe is smart if he gets his foot in the *funeral parlor* door. It's a place to show respect (that special mob virtue) and be introduced to important people. Wakes are both social and business occasions. It's nice, although it's really not necessary, to have known the dead guy. Just being there is what counts.

It may seem unusual for a red-blooded young man to choose to spend so much of his free time in dimly lit neighborhood funeral parlors, but these are the places where the major decisions pertaining to his future are made. Like a seat at the grown-ups' table at Thanksgiving, a spot in the Family opens up only with the death of one of its members. The only difference is that, luckily, in *this* Family you generally don't have to wait for people to die of natural causes. The clever wannabe will be there when the "books" open up, in line for promotion.

If he's done all his homework, the

wannabe will begin to get regular "work" with the Family and officially go "on the record" as an *associate*. When he proves himself, he stands a pretty good chance of achieving the highest of all honors: getting sworn in to the Family—in official mobspeak, "getting made" or "getting his button." The would-be wiseguy doesn't actually know if or when it will happen, but he can generally gauge Family opinion, just by some of the work he's assigned to perform. One future hit-man knew he'd made it when he was asked to go along on a "job." He accompanied his uncle, who proceeded to "whack" somebody. On another occasion, he was handed a gun and told to go along with the group. That "job" turned out to be an armored car heist.

Not all associates are officially brought into the fold. Some are barred because they aren't of the right heritage, and some prefer to remain "independent contractors." And of those who are eligible, not all succeed. Take the case of Tommy Lombardi. His friend didn't do a very good job of guarding the proceeds of a $50,000 liquor heist. The stash somehow disappeared, and underboss Aniello Dellacroce angrily directed Tommy and his henchman to make good on it—in cash. Now, loyalty and revenge are honorable mob traits, but Lombardi went about displaying them in all the wrong ways. He took a machine gun and decorated Dellacroce's social club with bullet holes. No one was hurt, but a week later Tommy Lombardi got "whacked."

Mob Morality

The cardinal virtues of the wiseguy are:

Greed: The granddaddy of them all. If he doesn't understand this, he shouldn't even bother.

Pride: No wiseguy has ever been known to be humble about the killing he made at the track or how he impressed his goumada last Friday night.

"Big Pete" Chiodo: Archetype

Envy: Instills motivation for obtaining the finer things in life by taking them away from other people.

Gluttony: *(See left)* A mobster can never have enough—whether it's money, mistresses, or macaroni.

Sloth: The wiseguy learns to delegate so he can concentrate on important matters, like eating and playing cards.

Lust: Necessary for pursuit, acquisition, and maintenance of a goumada. A girlfriend sure helps take the wiseguy's mind off business problems.

Anger: Provides convenient justification for anything, from breaking the plate-glass window of Vinny's Pizzeria because he's not paying his "vig," to breaking Vito's legs because he's been talking too much. Most primitively expressed by the mob wife upon discovery of the goumada.

Chapter Two

Having It "Made"

Having It "Made"

The lucky associate who has played his cards right and whose timing is good is now ready to be sworn in to that all-male bastion of organized crime, La Cosa Nostra. He is about to be "made." In the best mob tradition, you're supposed to pretend you don't know the biggest day of your life has arrived, but you dress in your Sunday best all the same. Al D'Arco, once an acting Boss and now one of the government's favorite mob witnesses, knows firsthand: "Well, you are not supposed to understand it, but they told you to get dressed, you surmise that you were going to be made a member."

The ceremony is deadly serious—after all, infringements on the oath are punishable by expulsion from the land of the living—but getting to the chosen site, for example, is almost comic in its labyrinthine complexity. D'Arco reports:

> *In the Bronx we switched cars and we were met by Mr. Manzo, Frank Manzo, and a fellow named Sally Bow, and we got in Sally Bow's car, it was a Cadillac, and we drove around, what they call "cleaning," making sure we had no tail.*
>
> *We squared blocks and, you know, drove around streets slow, and made fast turns, and just, in general just to make sure there was no surveillance on the car to know where we were going. We did that for about nearly a half hour.*

As an added precaution, the locale varies: an apartment over a funeral home, a social club, Aunt Mary's dining room, Tommy Flounderhead's finished basement.

When everyone has arrived, the ceremony begins. Actual inductions can range from the grandiose and ceremonious to the extremely blunt, but they all include:

1. Introductory Remarks. The head of the Family makes a speech impressing upon those gathered

See No Evil, Hear No Evil

Al D'Arco:

Well, I asked, do I know why I was there, and I knew why I was there, but you are not supposed to say why you are there. So I said, "no," I don't know why I'm there. They said, "Well, you are here and you are going to become a member of this family. Do you accept that? Do you have any objections?" I says, "no."

Sammy "The Bull" Gravano:

He asked me if I knew what I was doing there. I told him no. He asked me to look around, if I knew everybody that was sitting down at the table. I told him I knew them. He told me that this was a society, and he was about to induct me as a made member in the Gambino Family.

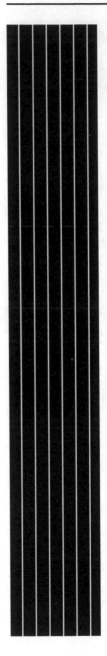

the solemnity of the occasion. Here's Raymond Patriarca's eloquent opening statement:

> We're all here to bring in some new members into our family and, more than that, to start maybe a new beginning. Put all that's got started behind us. 'Cause they come into our family to start a new thing with us. Hopefully, that they'll leave here with what we had years past. And bygones are bygones and a good future for all of us. I'll...and I'll greet you later. (Applause)

2. Official Opening. Sometimes the consiglieri will act as master of ceremonies—sometimes the Boss takes charge of the whole affair. In the time-honored tradition, he'll intone the following: *In onore della Famiglia, la Famiglia e' aperta.* (In honor of the Family, the Family is open.)

3. Introductions. It's important that everyone at the ceremony know each other—because they may have to kill each other later. Joseph Russo explains it this way: "Most of us know most of them, but some of us don't know any of these."

Got that?

4. Establishing Loyalty.

The inductee is asked whether he would be willing to kill his nearest and dearest to protect the honor of the Family. "You got any brothers, Carmine?" And: "Your mother's dying in bed and you have to leave her because we called you, it's an emergency. You have to leave. Would you do that, Carmine?"

Even Carmine's mother will have to wait.

5. The Oath.

The associate is asked to repeat the solemn vow so that at least he'll understand why he's been instructed to do away with his loved ones. At least he *may* understand—if it's in Italian, it's only sometimes translated. The oath, due to comprehension and memory deficiencies, generally proceeds one or two words at a time: *Io, Carmine.* (I, Carmine.) *Voglio.* (Want.) *Entrare.* (To enter.) You get the idea.

6. The Pricking of the Trigger Finger.

In the best boy's tradition, the associate now becomes a "brother for life." Peter Chiodo said there was a gun and a knife on the table for his occasion. It was a bit less elaborate for Al D'Arco; they pricked his finger with a safety pin.

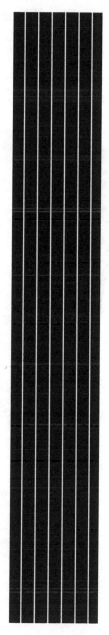

7. The Burning of the Holy Card.

Those present pass around a burning devotional card while saying, "*Come si bruscia questa Santa cosí si brucerá la mia anima.*" (As burns this Saint so will burn my soul.) One prominent Mafia funeral director recalls being asked for some holy cards "without the f——n' plastic on 'em." Wakes are the logical places to get the cards, since the wiseguys know there is now an opening in the Family. If the holy cards aren't available, the mobsters use whatever is on hand. Wiseguys have been known to use playing cards (often available!) or even toilet paper; in the former case a jack or queen can stand in easily for the necessary saint, while in the latter case considerably more imagination is required.

At this point, the wiseguys usually get a little sentimental. Sammy Gravano explained that after he took his oath from Boss Paul Castellano:

> *I kissed him on both cheeks. I kissed everybody. I went around the table and kissed everybody. I sat down. They got up. They locked hands. They unlocked hands. They made me get in the middle of it. They locked hands again, and told me, at that point, I was part of the brotherhood. I was a made member and I belonged.*

8. The Rules. The wiseguy is told in great detail what he can and cannot do, although he comes to learn that nobody ever really abides by the rules. While violations are punishable by death, the wiseguy will always try to get away with something. According to Al D'Arco:

> *We were instructed, there's no drug dealing, no securities and bonds, and no counterfeiting, and the penalty was death if we breached any of these offenses. We were told not to use our hands on other members, and to respect other members' families and treat them like they were your own family.*

D'Arco then goes on to explain how drugs were dealt all the time (he was arrested on narcotics charges) and that there was even a scheme to bleach smaller bills and turn them into larger denominations.

The biggest rule of all is *Omertá,* the proverbial vow of silence. Though it was rarely violated until recently, Al D'Arco as Acting Boss and Sammy Gravano as Underboss are the highest-level rats to come forward so far. It seems *Omertá* may be going the way of the burning holy card.

9. Closing Remarks. At the end of the ceremony hosted by Patriarca, Vincent Ferrara observed, "Only the f——n' ghost knows what really took place over here today, by God." How do we know? Because it was recorded by the FBI.

Chapter Three

The Upwardly Mobile Mobster

The Upwardly Mobile Mobster

Now that the associate has joined middle management in the diversified multinational corporation known as La Cosa Nostra, he faces the task of all ambitious young men—moving up the ladder. As in all corporations, this takes patience, good judgment, and a keen understanding of company politics. Perhaps more literally than in most fields, however, getting to the top is murder! Depending on his peculiar talents and proclivities, there are many career paths open to him. These include:

The Schlepper

A sort of mob valet, the schlepper handles all the Don's personal and family affairs. He drives the daughter to private school, picks up the dry cleaning. He has the key to the house. He must be able to take orders and keep his eyes and ears open and his mouth shut. Must be dutiful and obedient, with the willingness to carry out the most humiliating of tasks. ("Joey, Fifi needs to be walked.") You'd recognize him in surveillance photos as the guy holding the umbrella over the Boss's head when it rains. A hothead would quickly crash and burn on this career path.

The Corporate Hierarchy

DON

CEO

KING'S MAN

CONSULTANT,
PERSONAL ASSISTANT,
CONFIDANTE

CONSIGLIERI

COMPANY
COUNSEL/
TROUBLESHOOTER

UNDERBOSS

PRESIDENT

**CAPO
(A.K.A
"SKIPPER")**

DIVISION VICE
PRESIDENT

SOLDIER

MANAGER

The Hitman

Considered the riskiest route up the ladder because it involves the ultimate dirty work of the Family. The hitman must be able to operate well under pressure (which means not throwing up or fainting at the sight of blood) and he must be an excellent shot. If he ends up missing or merely injuring his intended targets, he could end up being a target himself. Hitmen are a truly special breed, and applicants are instructed to check their conscience at the door.

The Driver/Bodyguard

He's with the Don from first thing in the morning until late at night (unless the Don is with his goumada). He must be quick with the Mercedes and even quicker with the .38 caliber he keeps neatly tucked in his waistband. He must also have a look that will scare the living daylights out of anyone who dares to take up the double-parked spot outside the restaurant where he drops off the Don. He also goes in first and gives the place the once-over for his employer. He'll even take the car to the local garage once a month and have it checked for "bugging" devices. And he must be able to provide light conversation for the Don's amusement, something like "Hey, Boss, did you get a load of the story in the f——-n' paper? Tony Pascucci's wife reported him missing."

The Earner

Always scheming and devising new and inventive ways to make money, the earner has an eye for profit and an ability to forge (and force) business partnerships. He also knows how to diversify, whether it's setting up a concrete-pouring company or

Fatal Phrases

Whack

Make your bones

Hit

Do the right thing/Do him

Ice

Do a piece of work

Off

Put out a contract on

Clip

Fit him with cement shoes (archaic)

Break an egg

Make him sleep with the fishes (archaic)

a window replacement business (the earner doesn't necessarily have to know a thing about these occupations). He must have a good working relationship with the union reps, meaning they know their legs will be broken unless they cough up the obligatory kickback. Profit-sharing goes like this: As long as the Boss gets his required percentage, the earner keeps the rest.

The King's Man

He's a lifelong friend who can sit with the Don in the modest surroundings of the social club, or the glitzy interior of the latest East Side restaurant, and reminisce about the windows they broke together and the parking meters they ripped off as kids. The king's man also shares professional and personal confidences, anything from where the Don is thinking of setting up his goumada to when one of his errant capos must get "whacked."

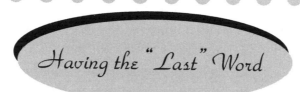

Having the "Last" Word

Running a giant conglomerate is a complicated task, and the Don, like any corporate CEO, knows he must delegate work and authority to lower management. But there is one issue that always rises to the top: The Don is the only person who can decide if someone has to get "whacked." It's a task not taken lightly, although it certainly acts as the ultimate remedy for just about any problem. The wise Don knows he can use the "hit" effectively in a number of ways.

As a Disciplinary Tool

For example: Louie DiBono had the unfortunate experience of upsetting John Gotti. Gotti, as head of the Gambino Family, became concerned when DiBono stopped "coming in" (attending the weekly meeting at the Ravenite Social Club). DiBono's behavior fueled suspicions that he was involved in a double-cross or, worse, that he had become a "rat." Gotti even gave DiBono a six-month grace period, which ended when police found DiBono's bullet-riddled body in the front seat of his car in the parking lot of the World Trade Center.

As Free Advertising

For example: The powers-that-be in the Lucchese crime family weren't about to give long-time soldier Bruno Facciola any grace period. When information leaked back to them, they determined it came from Facciola. The body of this "rat" was found with a canary stuffed in his mouth. The story was in the newspapers the next day, for all to see.

To Enhance Business

For example: Sammy "The Bull" Gravano complained to the Boss that his construction partner, Louie Milito, was having all sorts of tax and union problems. Contracts were dwindling, so Gravano asked permission to put his own "contract" out on Milito. It wasn't long before Milito disappeared and Gravano turned the company into a huge money-maker.

Methods of carrying out the "contract" are as varied as the Family business itself. Hitmen have their own individual styles. Tommy "Karate" Pitera initiated an elaborate ritual. After stripping naked, he dismembered his victims in bathtubs. Then he neatly packed the parts into several suitcases before dropping them off in a Staten Island bird sanctuary.

Man to Man

Tommy "Karate" Pitera isn't exactly one to brag, but he did share some mob morality with his girlfriend's son (perhaps misunderstanding her meaning when she asked him to "straighten [the kid] out").

PITERA: Find a spot in Staten Island. As long as you gut him, cut his lungs, body don't bloat.

JOSEPH PIRELLI, JR.: What do you mean, bloat?

PITERA: Bloat, push up.

PIRELLI: Oh.

PITERA: Cut his stomach, cut both lungs. Believe me, I did more than you ever f——n' heard, but I never did anything f——n' stupid. I never hurt anybody innocent. I never, I never did. All right? For me and you, for me and you to be f——n' drinking with me, and all of a sudden I take out a knife and stab you for no reason, I couldn't do it. For me to go and f——n' rip off an old lady's chains, I couldn't do it. I don't care who, a kid, I couldn't do it.

Reading for Fun and Profit

Tommy Karate's home library makes it clear that he's a man who loves his work. Here are some of the books found on his shelves:

Techniques with a Thirty-Six-Inch Baton
Advanced Short-Baton Techniques
The Challenge of Crime in a Free Society
Silencers from the Home Workshop
The Silencer Cookbook
An Infantry Man's Guide to Urban Combat
How to Get Anything on Anybody
Loompanics Unlimited: 1985 Main Catalog
The Hitman's Handbook
The 007 Travel Kit
The Black Bag Owner's Manual—Part Two:
        The Hit Parade (four copies)
The Perfect Crime and How to Commit It
Amnesty International: Report on Torture
Killer: Autobiography of a Hitman for the Mafia
Life without Fear
101 Sucker Punches
Keep 'Em Alive
The War of the Flea
Alcatraz: Island of Many Mistakes
Put 'Em Down, Take 'Em Out
Dead Clients Don't Pay
How to Disappear Completely and Never Be Found

Torture in the Eighties
Unarmed against the Knife
Gunfighting at Home and Related Subjects
Pocket Guide for Crime Scene Investigators
How to Perform Strong-Man Stunts
Behavior Modification
Exotic Weapons
How to Find Anyone Anywhere
Torture, Interrogation & Execution
The Anarchist Cookbook
How to Kill:

  Volume One (one copy)
  Volume Two (two copies)
  Volume Three (two copies)
  Volume Four (two copies)
  Volume Five (two copies)
  Volume Six (one copy)

Shooting to Live
The Anarchist Handbook
How to Rip Off a Drug Dealer
Getting Started in the Illicit Drug Business
The Outlaw's Bible
A Handbook of Anti Mau Mau Operations
Making Crime Pay
Brass Knuckle Bible (two copies)
Vigilante Handbook
French Foreign Legion Mines and Booby Traps
Close Shaves
Hitman: A Technical Manual for
  Independent Contractors

Conversation with a Hitman

The Mafia Handbook sat down and spoke with another hitman, Harry (the name has been changed to protect the guilty):

HANDBOOK: How do you feel about killing people for a living?

HARRY: It's no big deal. I've been around dead bodies all my life. My family's in the funeral business.

HANDBOOK: What was it like your first time?

HARRY: I was about eighteen years old. I had to kill a guy in Brooklyn. It took me so long to find him that I got hungry. So, after I shot him, I went and got something to eat.

HANDBOOK: How do you carry out a hit?

HARRY: I learn the guy's routine. I'll try to catch him on the street, maybe give him a flat tire or something, so he's standing still. Then I just go up to him and shoot him in the head.

HANDBOOK: Did a target ever give you a hard time?

HARRY: Once I shot a guy in the Bronx, but I had to dump him in Queens. I had to take him all the way across the Throggs Neck Bridge.

HANDBOOK: So you stuffed the body in the trunk?

HARRY: No, I propped him up in the passenger seat, and went through the toll booth. Nobody noticed a thing.

HANDBOOK: How else can you get rid of a body?

HARRY: If the victim isn't a made man, I'd just leave him there. But if he was a member of the Family, he'd have to disappear. In some cases, he'd end up with somebody else in the same casket.

HANDBOOK: What do you mean?

HARRY: They'd make a false bottom and slide the other guy underneath. The pallbearers at the funeral would get paid extra because they were carrying a heavier load.

The Hit Parade

There's always a reason why someone is targeted for a "piece of work." It could be as trivial as not opening the door fast enough for "Crazy" Charlie Imbroglio (everyone in the neighborhood knew Charlie had a short fuse). Or it could be as deadly serious as checking out Charlie's wife! In most cases, however, the reason is pure and simple: GREED. And greed has taken down the best of them:

Little Carmine Galante (5'3") got too big for his britches when he resumed leadership of the Bonanno Crime Family after a stint in prison. He wanted all the profits from the Family's lucrative drug operation. In the end, he got all the bullets that went flying across the patio of Joe and Mary's Italian-American Restaurant.

✝ ✝ ✝ ✝

Ashes to Ashes

Carmine Galante died with his boots on and a cigar in his mouth

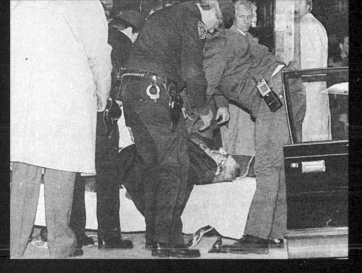

Some unhappy campers in the Gambino Crime Family didn't like Boss Big Paulie's brand of nepotism; they felt like stepchildren when it came to profit-sharing. So they branched out into the pharmaceutical industry (a.k.a. the drug trade). Paulie wanted no part of it; the upstarts wanted no part of Paulie. Guess who won?

While sitting in the barber chair, the ruthless chief of Murder Incorporated got "clipped" because he was playing too many angles. Albert Anastasia ticked off rival bosses by muscling in on their gambling operations in Cuba. He even had the nerve to charge a Mob membership fee! His membership expired October 25, 1957.

Nicked

Albert Anastasia on the floor of the barber shop of the Park Sheraton Hotel

✝ ✝ ✝ ✝

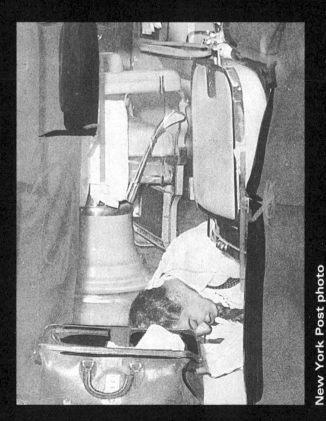

New York Post photo

NO APPOINTMENTS EVER BEFORE 11:00 A.M.

11:00 A.M.: Pick up car (1990 Cadillac Seville) at Gino's Autobody (false bottom being installed in trunk). Drive to deli for coffee and the *New York Post*. Check to see if Not Guilty won in the fifth at Aqueduct; check to see if police turned up Tony Pascucci's body yet.

12 NOON: Check in at social club; find out if they're still going to make Johnny "Fish Eyes" Forlano and put in a good word for him. Check with Skipper for business assignments.

12:30 P.M.: Shake down Vito for $500 "vig."

1:00 P.M.: Pick up "swag" from Tony's Ironworks. Make sure to ask for three "yard railings" (TVs) and fourteen "front gates" (VCRs). Make a call from pay phone on 13th Avenue to find out which catering halls want a piece of the latest liquor haul. Run into Tony's deli for prosciutto sandwich and a rice ball.

1:30 P.M.: Stop at Mama's house on Union Street. Have a bowl of *pasta fagioli* despite protestations you've just eaten.

2:15 P.M.: Go to the track. Lose $600. Threaten to rough up Funzie for giving you a bad tip on the seventh race.

5:30 P.M.: Go home, change clothes, see wife Angelina, eat a bowl of minestrone despite protestations you've just eaten.

6:00 P.M.: Return to club; head to midtown hotel for cocktails and "business" meeting on who "owns" the brick-layers union.

11:00 P.M.: Go to girlfriend Maria's apartment. Have a beer, watch the eleven o'clock news to see if police found Tony Pascucci's body yet.

NO APPOINTMENTS
EVER BEFORE 11:00 A.M.

11:00 A.M.: Maid serves breakfast—espresso and biscotti—and brings newspapers. Scan *The Wall Street Journal, The New York Times* Business section, and *New York Post* to see if police have turned up Tony Pascucci's body yet.

11:50 A.M.: Driver/bodyguard comes around with Mercedes.

12 NOON: Go to Angelo's Barber Shop for a shave, trim, and manicure.

1:00 P.M.: Go to legitimate business office, Father and Sons Imports Inc., in lower Manhattan. Make sure the "olive oil" is coming in.

2:00 P.M.: Stop at social club for lunch. Have the cook whip up linguini with clam sauce; meet with underboss and consiglieri about making Johnny "Fish Eyes." After lunch, take a "walk and talk" with underboss. Order schlepper to fill up Mercedes.

3:30 P.M.: To DeLisi's for a fitting of midnight blue, chalk-striped, double-breasted suit.

4:00 P.M.: To Jimmy's on Kings Highway for new tie to wear to granddaughter's christening.

4:30 P.M.: Call goumada, make plans to see her at her beachhouse tomorrow night.

5:00 P.M.: Return home, freshen up. Ask wife Rose if the kids are coming for dinner Sunday. Watch six o'clock news to see if police found Tony Pascucci's body.

7:00 P.M.: Business dinner at Pulcinella's with lawyer and capo Sally "Pencil Neck" Squiteri about pending racketeering indictment. Rear corner table with view of door. Order tomato salad, veal special, bottle of Brunatte Ceretto. Tip throughout meal.

Chapter Four

A Finger in Every Pie

A Finger in Every Pie

Like many multinational corporations, La Cosa Nostra prides itself on generating lucrative profits for its investors and employees. While these entities have the same aim and structure, the mob's methods of operation are just a bit different. Making as much money as possible while breaking a few legs is considered business as usual. Of course, in these ever-changing economic times, it's important for the leadership of each organization to take stock of their diversified enterprises. To that end, they've established a commission. At their meetings, the Bosses deliver status reports, compare notes, and iron out problems. So here in the corporate tradition is a general financial overview of New York's Five Families at work.

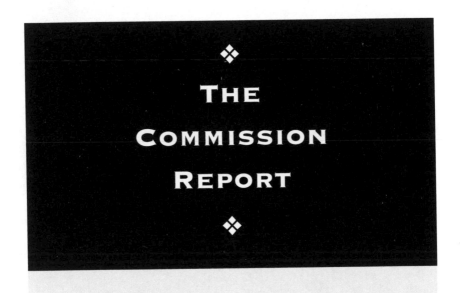

❖

THE

COMMISSION

REPORT

❖

THE BIG PICTURE

We at La Cosa Nostra are happy to report continued progress in making money the Family Way. Precedent for this practice exists as far back as biblical times, and we fully intend to carry on this venerable tradition. As a hedge against the vagaries of the economy and the ravages of inflation—to say nothing of interference from the federal government with the free exercise of capitalism—we have managed to become wholly diversified. Certain previously lucrative enterprises, such as hijacking, have been temporarily phased out in an effort to keep pace with the times. Since the unfortunate incident last February when one of our shipments, believed to contain lobsters destined for restaurants from Atlantic City to New York, turned out to contain $2,000,000 worth of Alka Seltzer, we have determined that the enterprise is too risky to be cost-effective. We have, however, consolidated certain operations and expanded others with a view to the future. In recent years one organization in particular has cut a successful path.

CONSTRUCTION

From the concrete-poured foundation to the electric socket in the completed penthouse suite, our integrated network of companies ensures the finished product. That's because our companies are utilized almost exclusively—otherwise there is no product at all.

Concrete is one of our most successful endeavors. It's been a shared business for years. In the early 1980s, we were responsible for 93 percent of all concrete poured in New York City. In recent years, government intervention has forced our most lucrative endeavors—

Certified, Transit-Mix, and Big Apple—to go the way of concrete shoes. But be assured that other firms are currently in the process of filling the vacuum.

Some outsiders might complain about our higher costs—specifically the 2 percent rate charged on all jobs costing under $2 million. We simply explain that it ensures a job completed without any problems.

PERSONNEL

We are extremely fussy about our employees and we dispense quickly with those who don't make the grade. Take the unfortunate case of Louie Milito. He was "dismissed" when Atlas Gem Steel wasn't surpassing prior profit margins. After the partnership (and Milito) was dissolved, Gem Steel earned nearly $1 million in 1989, up from $78,000 in the previous year.

And it is not above our chief officers to take on the smaller job. John Gotti has been on the payroll of ARC Plumbing as a salesman for many years. Not that he's ever sold pipes and fixtures. But he may have other talents with a monkey wrench. His modest occupation also allows for a multitude of tax shelters—as evidenced by his reported income over the past few years (see pages 82–83).

REAL ESTATE

Our holdings are extensive and diverse, catering to a client's every need. Our small storefront properties are perfect for meeting sites, money–laundering fronts, clearing-houses for stolen goods, and outlets for our vending machines. Each comes with the all–important back room, convenient for gambling, sit-downs, and private "contract" work. Our larger parcels provide the grounds for chop shops, swag storage, restaurants, and catering halls. Our warehouses are particularly useful as permanent drop-off points for unsavory customers. We advise against digging up the basement of any of the stated properties.

We are also discreet in our ownership. The ever-cooperative frontman puts his name on all leases, licenses, charters, etc., in order to protect the Family from any "nuisance" government litigation.

GARMENT INDUSTRY

Our motto is "We dress you up and shake you down." For the last sixty years, we have successfully encouraged manufacturers to use our trucks for the all-important and timely transport of goods in New York City's garment center. Under the successful stewardship of

Gambino Family Vice President Tommy Gambino, who oversees ten trucking firms, the business has flourished. We don't like to boast, since the government does it for us, estimating that our operation grosses over $100 million a year. Our clients have been most cooperative, and we make sure they are. After a phone call, or a "visit," rest assured they are convinced our service is worth just about any price. And any

JOHN GOTTI

SOURCE	1984	1985
W-2:		
ARC PLUMBING HEATING CORP.	$17,990.00	$21,910.00
CAPRI CONSTRUCTION CORP.	$13,000.00	$3,000.00
SCORPIO MARKETING INC.		
Total W-2 Wages	$30,990.00	$24,910.00
Other: 1099 Misc. Non-Employee		
Commissions	None	None
1099 Interest	None	None
1099 Dividends	None	None
1099B Sale of Stocks or Bonds	None	None
1099G Tax Refunds	None	None
1099R IRA Rollovers	None	None
W-2G Gamble Winnings	None	None
1098 Mortgage Interest Paid	None	None
5498 IRA Contributions	None	None
K-1 Partnership Income	None	None

prospective competitors are met by our "welcome wagon," whose members are predisposed to do whatever is necessary to bring the message home.

Unfortunately, at this juncture, our trucking operation is under government "reorganization." Due to extensive litigation, we have agreed to dismantle our interests (and pay out what the government refers to as a "fine," but what we prefer to call a "donation," of $12

1986	1987	1988	1989	1990
$11,400.00	$18,600.00	$26,000.00	$40,100.00	$41,600.00
			$59,182.00	$78,000.00
$11,400.00	$18,600.00	$26,000.00	$99,282.00	$119,600.00
None	None	None	None	None
None	None	None	None	None
None	None	None	None	None
None	None	None	None	None
None	None	None	None	None
None	None	None	None	None
None	None	None	None	None
None	None	None	None	None
None	None	None	None	None
None	None	None	None	None

million). But we are confident that we will resume our successful business practices at some future time.

UNION OPERATIONS

We could never be successful in our commercial operations if it wasn't for the cooperation of our friends in the unions. A $100,000 bribe is a worthy investment, if we know the official will allow us to bypass union regulations or put up no-show jobs. He'll also influence contract bids and price-fixing, and make entrées for our influence into new industries. For example, our presence in the window-installation union paved the way for our successful bids on lucrative city window-replacement contracts. Our take was two dollars each on over a million windows slated for work.

PHARMACEUTICAL INDUSTRY

This division spans the globe, to include the exotic locales of South America, Southeast Asia, and Sicily. Due to the sensitive nature of the product, we are discreet in our international distribution system. We've been known to transport the merchandise in espresso pots, sewer pipes, and furniture. On some occasions, we've placed the material between layers of pottery. We've even sent the goods in the guts of cattle.

Profits are conservatively estimated in the billions. The white powder variety provides most of the earnings. For example, our Southern representatives will pay $2,000 for a kilo of the coca plant product, which, after being cut many times, can fetch $30,000 on our local market.

Stringent regulations make domestic movement a little more difficult. And we've lost some key personnel to involuntary government custody. But we've also learned to cooperate, rather than compete, with other interested parties; for instance, we've offered the ambitious Asian entrepreneurs the use of our highly effective network—for a price. It's a way of keeping peace among competitors.

WASTE DISPOSAL

We've virtually cornered the market on commercial carting, by mapping out specified territories in the metropolitan area. The designated firms in those areas are free to control their prices—under our guidance. Our Long Island operation in the private carting sector reaps about $10 million a year.

And in this environmentally aware society, we've

entered into the toxic waste and recycling fields. For a fee, we collect and haul the goods away. Just don't ask us where we put it. Our friends at local landfills and dumpsites are happy to look the other way, if the price is right; and dissatisfied customers are cheerfully introduced to our latest line of trash compactors.

GAMBLING AND LOANSHARKING

The backbone of our entire enterprise, this is the most consistent money-maker, ensuring a guaranteed cash

① Tommy Ricciardi (Thomas Angelo) Born 5/
293 Vermont Avenue Lakewood N.J. Tom
② Martin Ralph Taccetta B- 5/2/5
25 Woodbine Road Florham Park N.J.
Mothers Condo 112 Ashley Bra
③ Michael Perna B 4/28/52 73 Pledg
④ Martin Taccetta 6 Timber CT. Flor
⑤ Michael Taccetta
⑥ Joseph Taccetta Uncle
282 E. Mt. Pleasant Ave Livingst
⑦ Angelo Taccetta Father 153 Cast
⑧ Martin Ralph Taccetta 5/2/5
N.J.
① Guisseppi Abate ×
⑤ Leonard Pizzolato Died 199
⑩ Michael Perna
¥ Andrew Licari
⁵ Michael Taccetta
⁶ Martin Taccetta
⁷ Tommy Ricciardi

John Lacar
Vic Cantil
Randy Delo
Danny Mian
Nicky Skins
Pat

Up to 7/18/   25,000 03 - less 25% = 18,750
Don   20,000 06   less 21% - 7,500
26,250 - 25% evo out 1,000 ea -
Don 15000 Revisance 8/70 + 15000 To
" 3000 L.I. P.V.
-6000 Bal Scala.   balance on 25 no 25% sp
" 1000 T. Pet. 7/20/90 ??
" 15000 Revisance 9/27/ 5000 J
evo out L.I.
8 Airel Rec.T. 10/1/90
" 7500 Hole (Any) 10,000 less 25% - 7
no split 25%
" 7500 John G. on 3 way split 11
3,750 (7000 less 25%) John G. 11/12/90
" 8,000 Markson (Hisl) John G. 1
" 4,400 John G. 12/1
" 5,000 John G. 12/15
" 30,000 Airport Tom. Pet. 12/18
" 2,000 X-Mas Gift 12/20
" 30,000 Airport Tom. Pet. 12/27
" 25,000 Picone 1/7
" 15,000 Scalmali 2/12
" 5,000 L.I. 2/12
" 6,700 Bronx Lux 3/13
" 6,700 (7000) Bronx Lux 3/17
" 6,000 (5000) Revisance 3/10
" 1,500 25% Revisance 3/19
Tal 244,150 Total 25% percent 7000=
PLUS

flow. Here the average Joe gets a chance to participate in our lucrative ventures. He doesn't have to be a successful businessman with a sterling financial record to secure a loan. Why go to the bank, when he can reach out for the local shylock? His late-payment penalty, however, is a meeting with a muscle-bound collection officer in a dark alley. And even though OTB parlors are found around virtually every corner, there isn't an outlet for betting on other professional sports. We provide the odds, the money, and our own hi-tech "parlors" with video screens, satellite dishes, and fax machines. Our

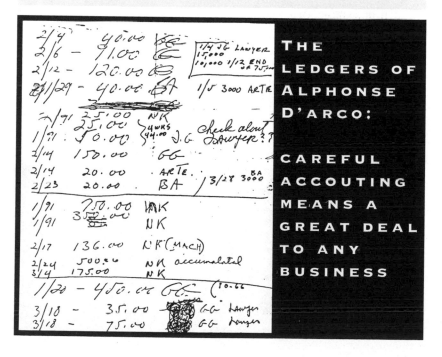

THE LEDGERS OF ALPHONSE D'ARCO:

CAREFUL ACCOUTING MEANS A GREAT DEAL TO ANY BUSINESS

"numbers" game is our own brand of lottery. We even rip off the numbers from the state game to set our own; the bets can be low (about a dollar) and the odds can be high (500 to 1). The best part of all this—the winner's earnings are tax-free. And in this era of rising unemployment, we can proudly say this venture puts thousands of people to work.

Despite the complexities of our holdings, our accounting methods are deceptively simple, so much so that they've been handed down by word of mouth for generations. Once in a while, however, an executive officer may feel compelled to make a few notations. For example, former President (Underboss) Alphonse D'Arco kept a ledger (see pages 86–87) for Lucchese CEO (Boss) Vic Amuso, who was temporarily forced to conduct business from out of town.

Chapter Five

Law and Disorder

Chapter Five

Law and Disorder

One of the

occupational inconveniences of a career in organized crime is the constant vigilance required to duck the long arm of the law. The wiseguy learns standard avoidance techniques early on—and years of practice sharpen his skills. But he can never be "100 percent sure," as Sammy the Bull would say, that he'll never get "pinched." So when he does, the wiseguy bows to necessity and hires a lawyer.

Hired Guns

The wiseguy's ambivalence toward this unavoidable evil is evidenced by mob parlance for a member of the legal profession, known as a "hard-on with a suitcase." A female attorney is graced with the charming moniker "half a hard-on with a suitcase." It certainly was a sore subject for John Gotti. In complaining to his top aides about all the money he was forced to shell out for legal representation for his associates, he was heard to comment: "You got Sammy, you got one hand in his pocket. You got both your hands in Joe Butch's pocket. Where does it end? Gambino Crime Family? This is the Shargel, Cutler, and whattaya call it Crime Family. . . . "

Gotti also referred to his just-mentioned and often-used attorneys as "Muck and F—k."

Bellying Up to the Bar

The three favorite mob witnesses are:

The "cooperating witness."
Generally a witness for the prosecution who develops a sudden case of amnesia. Inexplicable by medical standards, its onset is heralded by a large cash "gift" or a friendly visit by "Big Louie," who just happens to be carrying a baseball bat.

The "character witness."
Something of a character himself, he can be depended upon to sing the wiseguy's praises. The defendant is typically

described as a regular guy who minds his own business, supports local charities, attends his son's Little League games, and works tirelessly to keep crime out of his neighborhood.

The "disappearing witness."

A favorite, although difficult to characterize for obvious reasons.

If his witnesses fail him, the wiseguy has twelve more potential allies, but gaining their cooperation is fraught with its own set of difficulties. For example, one mobster tried to leave a threatening message on a juror's front door, but his messengers went to the wrong house and wound up leaving the note on the door of an FBI agent who lived on the same block.

The Jury Box

Top 10 Excuses Cited by Potential Jurors to Avoid Selection for Mafia Trial

10) Reluctance to postpone much-anticipated root canal.

9) Never a complaint, none whatsoever, with quality of work done at defendant's laundry establishment.

8) Cannot, in good conscience, leave elderly goldfish unattended.

7) In the event of guilty verdict, cost of lifetime, round-the-clock security would be prohibitive.

6) Once attended all-day fly-casting seminar at Bergin Hunt and Fish Club.

5) Evidence notwithstanding, inclined to see the good in all people.

4) Can't swim.

3) Used to hang around Ravenite Social Club swapping pesto recipes with John Gotti.

2) Instructed by my dog not to.

1) Have trouble distinguishing right from wrong when pants are wet.

If he can't stand the thought of going to trial or the prospect of life in prison without parole, the wiseguy has another option. He can become a member of that ever-expanding club—the RAT PACK.

Rat Patrol

The mob's worst enemy and the government's most valuable possession, the "rat" does the unthinkable when he cooperates with law enforcement. He's violating *Omertá*, the vow of silence he took when he got "made." Compared to life in prison, however, cooperation doesn't look too bad. In exchange for his testimony, the wiseguy must serve significant jail time, but that can be reduced depending on how cooperative he is. Sammy the Bull scored big time: He brought down John Gotti and Colombo Boss Vic Orena. "Little" Al D'Arco and "Big" Pete Chiodo earned points by helping to convict Vic Amuso, another crime family Boss.

EPITOME OF A RAT WHO LIES

SAMMY "THE LIAR" GRAVANO

Flyer circulated at John Gotti's 1992 murder and racketeering trial

If he sings right on key, the canary will get the red-carpet treatment—if you call hanging around with a bunch of investigators acting as twenty-four-hour security a good time. While he's in custody, he's hidden at various locations—a fancy hotel, a beachfront condo—and he's billed as a "star" witness, getting headlines at sensational trials. But once the party's over, he gets thrown back into the real world—with a new identity in hand. He is now placed in the renowned Witness Protection Program.

A Rat by Any Other Name

A canary
A snitch
A stool pigeon
"He's gone bad"
"He sings"
"He turned"
"He flipped"
"He dropped a dime" (archaic—a phone
call now costs twenty-five cents)

WITSEC

Getting into WITSEC is relatively easy for a renegade wiseguy, but staying in is probably the biggest challenge of his life. Why? Because he has to do something he's never done before— live like a law-abiding citizen! Some get kicked out of the program. Many cheat. They just can't help themselves. A recent behavioral study shows that wiseguys in WITSEC salivate at the mere sight of a racing form.

He's forbidden to contact relatives and friends or go back to his old stomping grounds. So along with new shoes, a new suit, and a new place of residence in some God-forsaken town in the middle of nowhere, the government provides a list of do's and don'ts to help him stay on the straight and narrow:

When what can now be described as the Man of Dis-Honor joins the Witness Protection Program, he must undergo a necessary but torturous deprogramming to unlearn all the crooked behavior he's crafted to a criminal science over the course of his lifetime. For the deposed delinquent, a day in WITSEC is like a day in a mental institution—just short of the straitjacket. His *re*-programming includes the following:

1. Watching a hundred hours a month of

"Father Knows Best,"
"Ozzie and Harriet,"
and "The Donna Reed Show"

2. Consuming huge daily quantities of:

apple pie

macaroni and cheese

franks on a roll with mustard
and sauerkraut

any type of fast food besides pizza

lemonade/diet soda

3. Agreeing to wear:

Bass Weejuns

suspenders

pants with cuffs

boxy, single-breasted suits

sweats bearing the name of
an Ivy League school

How to Stay in WITSEC:

DO:

1. Join the Kiwanis Club.
2. Keep in touch with your federal sponsor.
3. Help a little old lady across the street.
4. Say "good morning" to the local police officer.
5. Join the church choir.

DON'T:

1. Volunteer to organize the gambling tent at the county fair.
2. Send cousin Vinny a postcard saying "Wish you were here."
3. Shake the little old lady down.
4. Tell the officer you'll make it worth his while if he tells you where you can find some "action."
5. Tell them about your recent "singing" experience.

4. Engaging in such activities as:

going to the mall

driving a Volkswagen

attending a baseball game and
participating in "The Wave"

going on a foxhunt

walking a golden retriever named Rover

5. Accepting daily visits from:

the U.S. marshal assigned to him

the den mother
who will make sure
he mows the lawn,
makes his bed,
cleans his room,
and does his homework
for his grammar school
equivalency diploma.

Home Away from Home

For less serious offenses, or for those who balk at joining the Rat Pack, there's cable TV, handball courts, a library, boot-legged liquor, and a vegetable gar-den—we're not talking about the Don's five-acre spread in northern New Jersey, we're talking about The Penitentiary. If you counted up all the days in a wiseguy's life, you'd find that he's probably spent more time sitting in the "joint," as it's affectionately called, than he has at his own dinner table. But to the wiseguy, it's no big deal. He doesn't view his time behind bars as punish-ment; it's more like a stepping stone—part of the process of earning a respectable place in the Family. It's also regarded as a status symbol because in the classic manner of mob one-upmanship, one wiseguy

Heavy hitters
Warden's Class of '73 at
Lewisburg Penitentiary

will inevitably ask the other, "Where'd you do your time?" Of course, the preferred answer is that you were in the federal facility; it not only indicates the seriousness of the crime but it reveals that your stay was passed in quality accommodations. No wiseguy ever likes to hear another wiseguy snicker, "Hey, how'd the STATE get you?!"

The resourceful wiseguy makes the best of what, for him, is not exactly a bad situation. It's con-

ceivable that he even views prison as a sort of sleepaway camp, or the college dorm experience he never had. For some unexplained reason, prison officials house mobsters in the same barracks, and in some of the low-security pens, the rules are pretty loose. So the wiseguy can roam the grounds, watch television, make phone calls (collect)—in effect, he can conduct business, even though he has to go about it with just a bit more discretion.

When he gets to the pen, one of the first things the wiseguy does is get himself a job. It keeps him busy, and it keeps him in the good graces of the warden. Some of the most desirable jobs are:

chaplain's assistant
library clerk
teacher of English as a second language
warden's cook

Rest assured, the wiseguy will NEVER take on a job that's very physical. He'll pay someone else to do the work instead.

Of course in prison, money never changes hands. But the inmate who ends up cleaning the toilets will probably find a sudden increase in his commissary account; or his wife will tell him that a visitor identifying himself only as "The Snake" recently dropped off a shopping bag full of cash at her door.

Even if he's looking at a long stretch, that doesn't mean there isn't plenty for a wiseguy to do. For exercise there is the ever-popular handball game, and softball competition gets pretty intense (think of all the experience they have with baseball bats!). There is also a weightlifting room, and in federal penitentiaries in sunnier locales like Georgia or Alabama he can sit outside and get a tan. Perhaps that's why mob investigators wryly note that mobsters often look better AFTER they get out than before they went in.

A telltale sign of a wiseguy who has done his time is the habit of walking endlessly around the same square block in his neighborhood day in and day out. It's reminiscent of the hours he spent walking around the prison track.

From Cop to Capo— Going Undercover

You don't have to be a real wiseguy to learn to look, act, and—most important—think like one. But it helps if you're trying to make Vinny "The Fish" the catch of the day in an undercover investigation. Achieving the quintessential wiseguy persona is instrumental in generating the trust necessary between you and your criminal target. Here are some inside tips from one man who traded in his holster and handcuffs for a manicure and a Mercedes:

1. **Establish camaraderie (so your target says, "Hey, he's just like me!"). If you want to earn his trust, have him catch you doing something illegal—like stuffing a "corpse" in the trunk of a car (oops!) or threatening to kill somebody (all staged, of course). Never let on that you**

know he sees/hears this. Your target will be very happy to learn that you're both on the same wavelength.

2. Establish fear (so your target says, "Hey, don't f—k with this guy!"). Have him catch you in a conversation in which you discuss the "disappearance" of someone who didn't deliver the goods. Or insult your target by putting him in a position that makes him look bad (without his knowing you did it, of course).

3. Establish the ability to earn (so your target says, "Hey, we can make money with this guy!"). Greed is the common denominator in any organized crime endeavor. The way to a wiseguy's heart is through his pocket.

4. Use props (so he says, "Hey, he hangs out at Caesar's in Vegas!"). You never know what kind of conversation/information you'll stimulate when you flash a matchbook cover, letterhead, businesscard, etc.

5. Never say the obvious—especially the word "murder" (so your target says, "Hey, he's a mother-f——n' cop!"). That's the dead giveaway, usually recognized when it's too late.

Chapter Six

Dressed to Kill

Dressed to Kill

Whether he's carrying out a hit or just ordering one, a mobster is under an obligation to look the part. Even though he set fire to his uni-

Reaching new fashion heights

form when he finally got out of Catholic grammar school (unfortunately while someone else was wearing it), he has nevertheless subscribed to the unwritten dress codes of the Family. After all, half the fun of being a goodfella is looking like one. Whether his look is cugine casual or classic mob chic depends on his current standing in the Family and how far he hopes to progress. Some mobsters may settle for less than sartorial splendor, but others find they look better and live longer as a well-turned-out wiseguy—because they've come to learn that Dressiness is next to Gotti-ness.

The Lean Cugine Quiz:

1. The cugine wears ten chains around his neck because:

    a. He wants to show off how much money his cugette spends on him.
    b. He wants to show off his connec-tions to the guys who pull off jewelry heists.
    c. He has to hide the three hickeys on his neck.

2. The cugette buys a dozen pairs of black Spandex tights because:

    a. There was a sale at The Mandee Shop.
    b. Why should she be different from any other cugette?
    c. Black makes her legs look thinner.

Correct answer to 1 and 2—
all of the above.

Mob Chic from Cradle to (Early) Grave

Cugine

Tank-top/muscle shirt (the smaller the better), Lee or Levi's jeans, sweatpants and open-laced Nike sneakers, a phalanx of gold chains with obligatory crucifix or head of Christ (gift from cugette), a signet ring ("gold knuckles"), shaved haircut, tattoo on forearm. For funerals, wakes, and weddings: black, pleated and pegged pants, white-on-white shirt, narrow black tie, black-and-white tweed sports jacket, black shoes with skinny laces or black moccasins, black socks.

Cugette

Midriff or tank-top blouse (the smaller the better), Jordache stretch jeans or black tights, multitude of gold chains with charms (gifts from cugine) and diamond-encrusted name-plate. Gold hoop earrings, additional studs (balls or hearts) in additional holes, diamond-encrusted signet ring, i.d. bracelet, ankle bracelet, high heels, earth-tone foundation (instant tan), matte dark red lipstick, coral blush, black eyeliner (above and below eye), black mascara, thinly tweezed eyebrows, BIG HAIR.

Soldier

Short-sleeved double-knit or Ban-Lon shirt, three buttons opened to expose chest hair. Tattoo on upper forearm from when he was in the service. Heavy gold chain around neck (religious medal worn when he goes to court), pinky ring on left hand, blue star sapphire, gold chain link bracelet (conspicuously displayed), Movado watch, black or brown pants (protruding gut precludes a belt), racing form in back pocket, woven leather moccasins, black socks. In shirt pocket: pack of (unfiltered) Camels, matchbook from Taj Mahal in Atlantic City with scribbled phone number of newly acquired business associate (no name attached), toothpick.

His Goumada

Black spandex tights, tunic top with studs and sequins from Gina's Glitz 'n' Glama (run by fellow goumada), jet black or frosted hair (varies semi–annually), large gold

The Soldier

The
Goumada

hoop earrings, not-so-big hair, five chains around neck with religious medal and charm holder, gold Piaget watch, black eyeliner and mascara, three-tiered eye shadow, tweezed brows, melon blush and matching lipstick, Louis Vuitton bag, black high-heeled boots, hot-pink nails with embedded jewel and painted design or decal.

His Wife

Floral print housedress, bouffant "do" set and styled weekly at BeautyRama, acrylic nails in red with jewel, decal, or design, large glasses with elaborate frames and Florentine or jeweled decoration, slip-on wedge shoes, wedding band, mother's ring with birthstones of her children, three gold chains with religious medal and "World's Best Mom" charm.

Dapper Don

Blow-dried hair, neatly coiffed, cut and trimmed every week, white-on-white shirt, hand-tailored double-breasted suit, silk hand-painted tie and matching pocket square, diamond horseshoe tie tack and matching cufflinks, diamond pinky ring on left hand, hand-sewn Italian loafers, see-through ribbed socks, cashmere overcoat, Rolex watch.

The Soldier's Wife

The Don's Goumada

Tasteful big hair, frosted makeup, year-round tan from condo in Florida or beach house at Jersey shore, eighteen-karat-gold hand-designed jewelry, necklace, earrings, bracelets, and rings with matching stones. Low-cut, clingy wraparound dress from designer outlet store in Secaucus or Madison Avenue shopping spree, frosted nail "tips" in shade matching dress and makeup, white fox coat.

The Don's Wife

Short hair "done" weekly at Madison Avenue salon, eighteen-karat-gold jewelry in less bulk than goumada's, wedding band, mother's ring with birthstones of her children, Cartier watch, own nails done in muted shade, designer clothes in conservative styles, suitable for part-time job or volunteer work at local hospital/charity.

Retiree

Peaked hat, cigar firmly entrenched in mouth, polyester-blend polo shirt with T-shirt underneath, cardigan vest (he feels the chill at his age), racing form in pocket,

The Retiree

double-knit pants, moccasin shoes (so he doesn't have to bend over and tie them), one gold chain with religious medal, worn gold pinky ring.

The Retiree's Wife

Heavy-set in housedress topped with full-length apron, hair gone completely gray, own nails, manicured (some habits die hard), with frosted pink polish, slippers, wedding band, grandmother's ring with five birthstones, several gold chains hung with religious medal and "#1 Grandmother charm," diamond earrings.

His Girlfriend (some habits never die)

Some wiseguy's widowed sister, usually from the old neighborhood. For appearance, see above.

As soon as the wiseguy begins earning, he earns the right of introduction to the tailor. He'll shed those NBO and He-Man styles faster than he can run from the cops during a gambling raid.

The Mob Tailor comes highly recommended, specifically because of his terrible memory. And, of course, he wants to ensure a happy clientele; mobsters are certainly steady customers, so he caters to that little extra need, like the secret pocket in the sleeve for the roll of cash or policy slips, or that patterned lining that makes other goodfellas say, "Yo, nice lining." Mobsters are also big tippers, but they counterbalance their outlay by shaking the poor tailor down for an extra belt or a second pair of pants for that suit. The tailor can hardly afford to argue. Here are a few of his rules to (literally) live by:

123

Mob Tailor Do's and Don'ts

DO:

1. Offer to press the current suit the wiseguy is wearing as he gets fitted for another one.
2. Forget that the Don's nephew was in the shop earlier that day.
3. Throw in a belt made of the same material as the suit, and remember to add the gun loop.
4. Expect a big tip.
5. Expect to be invited to the nephew's wedding and provide a large voluntary cash gift.

DON'T:

1. Ask the wiseguy his name or what he does for a living.
2. Suggest vents in the jacket or cuffs on the pants.
3. Ask for a credit card.
4. Complain when Paulie "Jello" Arturi comes in to have his trousers let out for the fifth time.
5. Snicker at the wannabe's request for a sharkskin suit.

Winners of the "No—Belt" Prize

Mobmobiles

Cugine

**IROC Camaro—black
Trans-Am—white with blue stripe
Mustang GT—black or red**

Big red bow or cornu *hanging from rearview mirror. Floor and seats littered with fast-food wrappers, empty bottles of Budweiser. Baseball bat in trunk (for those impromptu games).*

Soldier

**nondescript 1985 Oldsmobile
Cutlass Supreme
1990 Cadillac in some discreet color
Mercedes-Benz, white**

St. Christopher or Sacred Heart magnetic statue on dashboard, box of union business cards in glove compartment, racing form on floor of backseat with three-day-old New York Post. *Baseball bat in trunk (for taking a few swings), .38 with serial number filed off in secret compartment.*

Capo

Mercedes-Benz, black, with tinted windows
Jeep Cherokee with tinted windows

On backseat, folder containing paperwork for new cement company partnership. Bottle of Tuscany cologne in glove compartment for those quickie visits to the goumada. Change of clothes in Hartmann suitcase in trunk in case business dictates an overnight stay in Atlantic City. Golf clubs in trunk (useful even off the links).

Boss

Mercedes or Lincoln Town Car, black, with tinted windows

Portable bar stocked with Chivas Regal in rear, copy of Playboy in side magazine panel (to keep the driver occupied while he waits), The Wall Street Journal, The New York Times *on backseat.*

"Speak, That I Shall Know Ye"

As integral to being a wiseguy as looking the part is sounding the part. Because mobsters tend to express themselves more eloquently through gestures than through words, the essence of mobspeak is simplicity—with a liberal sprinkling of obscenities for punctuation. A mobster doesn't need a sophisticated vocabulary to communicate effectively, and he usually screws it up if he tries. Take, for instance, Angelo Ruggiero, speaking with attorney Michael Coiro about a colleague's jail sentence (harder to ignore than the grammatical variety):

RUGGIERO: Because, let's assume he done the nine because three or four.
COIRO: Yeah.
RUGGIERO: Ship him over to the feds.
COIRO: Right.

RUGGIERO: Unless they aggravate the sentence, I don't know.

COIRO: Yeah.

RUGGIERO: Agg—aggravate.

COIRO: Aggregate.

RUGGIERO: Aggregate.

COIRO: Yeah.

The wiseguy knows he can get his message across with just a few key words and phrases. Time-honored expressions like "Know what I mean?" and "Do what you gotta do" are instrumental in all of his social or business conversations. And no wiseguy is ever going to misinterpret the meaning of "c—ksucker," "motherf—ker," and "hard-on," just a few of their favorite exclamations. Wiseguys never have trouble understanding one another, but for the puzzled layperson, or the FBI agent who may be listening in on a wiretap, here's a helpful primer. Oh, and pay attention. There will be a test.

January 4, 1990, Government-Recorded Conversation Between John Gotti and Frank Locascio

FRANK LOCASCIO: Yeah, if I might—

JOHN GOTTI: Go ahead.

LOCASCIO: —suggest four and three.

GOTTI: Who?

LOCASCIO: Make four, and then in a few weeks you, you put on another three.

GOTTI: No, here's what I'm saying.

LOCASCIO: Or, or go all five and —

GOTTI: The reason why I said the five—

LOCASCIO: Four and three I'm saying 'cause—

GOTTI: Yeah, I know what you're saying. I, I—here's what I'm—

LOCASCIO: Instead of making it five and two.

Translation Quiz

The subject of this conversation is:

a. an addition lesson
b. a baseball card swap
c. a meeting of the Family's chief financial officers

Answer: None of the above. According to the government translation, both men are talking about "opening the books" and "making" a few more members of the Family.

April 25, 1982, Government-Recorded Conversation Between Angelo Ruggiero and Vic Amuso

RUGGIERO: Uh, Johnny, I think he's gonna come here Monday night. Did he tell ya?

AMUSO: No.

RUGGIERO: He's comin' in Monday night. He's gotta see Christie. Something about that which Christie spoke to Neil about, or if he can't but he's gotta go to a wake first, so what time does Christie stay here, huh?

AMUSO: Christie.

Translation Quiz

What time does Johnny arrive?

Answer: Ask Christie.

January 4, 1990, Government-Recorded Conversation in Apartment over Ravenite Social Club

JOHN GOTTI: Don't you know why they ain't got the balls, too? I told them yesterday, I told them why. That's why Tommy was laughing. Ah, ask Tommy. "You don't get up and holler when you could because nothin' you couldn't do it. You can't even come to court six hours? You write a stay and you're out automatically. They got for six hours, tops, they keep you. You don't wanna do it because, you c—ksucker, you know and I know that they know that you're taking the money under the table."

Translation Quiz

Who is ripping Gotti off?

Answer: Another hard-on with a suitcase, of course (see Glossary).

Actions Speak Louder Than Words

Sometimes up to 50 percent of a conversation is conducted without either wiseguy actually saying a thing because they're employing the time-honored Mob Sign Language System. The system has been one of the most effective methods of making a point while defying both wiretaps and surveillance. It takes careful observation and practice to master the gestures. It's even harder to decipher them because one movement can often suggest several different things. As in the rest of life, context is everything. Here are the basics:

Sign Language:

Those

Little

Gestures

That

Mean

So

Much!

1. The Kiss can mean:

a. Hey, how ya' doin'?
b. You're a "friend of ours."
c. You're a dead man.

2. The Adjustment (hand going inside opened jacket of double-breasted suit) can mean:

a. He's relocating the .38-mm. "bulge" in his waistband.
b. He's relocating another "bulge."

3. The Shrug can mean:

a. Hey, Boss, I didn't know the
$50,000 liquor haul disappeared,
I swear on my kids!
b. That's too bad about Tony
Pascucci. We all gotta
go sometime.

4. Hand-to-Mouth (covering the mouth with the hand while speaking) can mean:

a. He's telling underboss Tony
"Fats," sitting at his right, that he
wants to put a contract out on
Ralphie "Snake Eyes," who
happens to be sitting at his left.
b. In court, he doesn't want some
smart-ass lip-reading reporter to
find out he's telling his lawyer that
the judge is a f—n' hard-on.
c. There was too much garlic in the
shrimp scampi he had for lunch.

5. Palm Press (hands together, almost as if in prayer, shaken back and forth) can mean:

a.   What am I gonna do with you, Frankie? You only shot him, you didn't kill him!

b.   Frankie, I'm sorry, I have no other choice—you know I gotta do what I gotta do.

c.   Jerry, you see what happened to Frankie? Now, you gonna do things my way, or what?!

6. The Touch (hands extended, fingers and thumb touching on each hand, facing up) can mean:

a.   He's whining to another goodfella that his weekly dice game has been slow.

b.   He's telling his goumada that he canceled their date for the third straight time because he had to go to his kid's Parent Night at school.

c.   He burned his fingers on a plastic-coated holy card during the initiation ceremony.

7. The Hitch (hands tucked in pants waistband, pulling them up) can mean:

a.   He's getting ready to take a "walk and talk" around the block of the social club.

b.   He ate too much pasta for lunch at Joe Butch's restaurant.

c.   His "piece" just fell down the leg of his pants.

8. The Gun (index finger extended, thumb bent to look like a gun) can mean:

a.   He's only kidding.

b.   Then again, maybe not.

9. The Curse (hand placed in crook of elbow of other arm) can mean:

a.   F—k you!

b.   You're f—ked!

c.   That's the last time you f—k with me!

The "Thing" Is the Thing

When he is having a conversation, the wiseguy's goal is to be as ambiguous as possible while still making sure he's getting his message across. His special brand of dialogue is a nearly equal mixture of words and gestures. The most useful word for maximizing ambiguity is "thing." In fact, the soon-to-be-published manual *The Wiseguy's Guide to Word Usage and Syntax* lists "thing" (apart from expletives, of course) as the most common word in the mob vocabulary. Here are some of its myriad meanings:

Thing (thing) n.

AN OBJECT—as in "I gotta pick up this *thing* [a gun, a haul of stolen goods, an assignment] at Jerry's."

MONEY—as in "I gotta collect the *thing.*"

AN ACTION—as in "Do the right *thing* by him."

AN ACT OF VIOLENCE—as in "We're doing this *thing* tonight."

Matching Quiz

Test your decoding ability by matching one "thing" with another:

1. a "loaf" of bread
2. a "dime"
3. "goin' south"
4. "escarole" or "cabbage"
5. getting "chased"
6. "this thing of ours"
7. "knocked down"
8. "tomato"
9. "I swear on my mother's eyes!"
10. "a friend of ours"

a. a good-looking cugette
b. making something or someone disappear
c. whatever it is, it's a lie
d. demoted in rank
e. a kilo of cocaine
f. a made man
g. La Cosa Nostra
h. $1,000
i. money
j. being run out of the Family

Answers: 1e, 2h, 3b, 4i, 5j, 6g, 7d, 8a, 9c, 10f.

When a mobster finds he must yield to necessity and string a few words together to form a sort of sentence, he carefully chooses those words to convey a symbolic rather than a literal meaning. In such cases, the wiseguy employs the classic Mob Conversation Code. For instance, Johnny "Wall Eyes" should be able to figure out that if Carmine tells him it's six o'clock when it's actually noon, it means that he just scored on a haul of six thousand suits.

Music to Talk By

Wiseguys want to be heard, but only among themselves. Since time immemorial, they've devised ways of getting around bugging devices. When investigators eavesdropped on conversations at the Bergin Hunt and Fish Club, they were confounded by a constantly running faucet. Authorities also planted a bug in a widow's apartment above the Ravenite Social Club, where John Gotti met with his henchmen. Not only did it pick up the most incriminating of conversations but it also offered a clue to the Dapper Don's musical tastes. Strains of "Mona Lisa" could be heard as Gotti and his aides were comparing the strength of their Family with that of another. They discussed making new members to the tune of "O Solo Mio." And, perhaps most appropriately, they complained about the fees of their often-used lawyers to the song "Love Is Blue."

Songs

and

"Sotto Voce"

Ain't Misbehavin'

It's a Sin to Tell a Lie

Keepin' Out of Mischief Now

Straighten Up and Fly Right

Money Makes the World Go Round

The Best Is Yet to Come

My Way

Anything Goes

The Joint Is Jumpin'

Things That Make You Go "Hmmmm"

Instead of listening to music, the

wiseguys often tune the radio to an all-news station; not only does the talk drown out their own, but they get up-to-the-minute information on the latest arrests, indictments, and track results, as well as whether the police found Tony Pascucci's body.

Chapter Seven

Getting Them Where They Live

Getting Them Where They Live

Be it grand or ever so humble, there is certainly no place like a wiseguy's home. It's more than just a place where he can hang his hat—and hide his .38. It reveals as much about him as the car he drives or the company he keeps.

Hide nor Hair

Stash locations aren't reserved solely for the living room. Wiseguys have been known to store their cash behind the baby's crib or in plastic-lined duffel bags buried in the backyard. Thousands of dollars' worth of coins from vending machines end up in suitcases in the garage (who's going to steal those?—no one can even pick them up!). Sometimes a mobster relies on a friend, a relative, or an "unconnected" person whom he trusts for help. And sometimes it's not just cash, drugs, or guns that he's trying to hide. Joey tells his mother he's in the carpet business to explain why he has to store a rolled-up remnant in her basement every once in a while. When she presses him for details, all he does is mumble incoherently about a few "dead" orders.

Depending on his ego and whom he wants to impress (or evade), the look of the Mobster's Manor can range anywhere from the seemingly simple to the gaudily grandiose. Take, for instance, the Staten Island mansion of former Gambino boss "Big" Paul Castellano, whose home was, literally, his castle. The lavish estate was built on the borough's highest hill and dubbed the White House not just because it looked like the one in Washington, but because, as Boss of Bosses, Castellano headed his own criminal empire. But fancy pools and manicured gardens weren't for the likes of Lucchese underboss Alphonse D'Arco. He and his family lived in a rented apartment in Manhattan's Little Italy section, and in the true mob tradition of getting away with something for nothing, he doctored some documents so that the government subsidized part of his rent!

The facades may differ, but the interiors of goodfellas' homes are remarkably similar—an amazing mixture of the tacky and the traditional, the ornamental and the functional. Your chances of finding that Capodimonte porcelain floral arrangement are good, whether you're visiting the home of a newly made member or that of the Don. The Don's wife probably has the $15,000 four-foot-high version sitting on top of her china closet in the formal dining room. The new member's wife has the smaller version with a hollow bottom where her husband hides the hot cash.

However, it's the subtle accoutrements of the Mob Manor that truly distinguish this home from any other:

1. Quilted/tufted couch with covered buttons; red-on-red patterned upholstery. Plastic slipcovers.
2. Mirror over couch, beveled, or with ornate gold trim.
3. Two gold, crushed-velvet chairs. Plastic slipcovers. Crocheted doilies on top.
4. Mediterranean-style, single-drawer end tables. Secret compartment behind drawer to hide .38.
5. Lamps with hanging crystal teardrops, plastic-covered lampshades.
6. Framed photographs on shelves in wall unit: Vinny, Joey, and Larry outside restaurant after being "made"; family at Baby Bruno's christening, Angelo and Tessie's wedding; Uncle Frankie before he went to prison.
7. On wall, gilt-framed wedding photo of Grandma and Grandpa Massina. Thin backing so there's room to hide small stacks of bills.
8. Red, flocked wallpaper.
9. Dark red, plush shag rug, covered in heavy traffic areas by plastic runners.
10. Forty-inch color TV, with knob broken from moving it off the back of the truck too fast.
11. VCR from last social club tag sale.

12. Tape library stocked with bootlegged versions of *Goodfellas, Married to the Mob, Prizzi's Honor, The Godfather 1–3, The Little Mermaid* for the kids.

13. Stereo system from Uncle Frankie before he went to prison.

14. Bootlegged CD library includes *Connie Francis's Love Songs, Dion and the Belmonts' Greatest Hits, Jay and the Americans' Greatest Hits, Enrico Caruso from La Scala,* the soundtrack from *The Godfather,* everything Frank Sinatra ever sang.

15. Glass coffee table, Capodimonte centerpiece, ashtray from last year's visit to Caesar's Palace, Las Vegas.

16. Wall unit including dog-eared editions of *Wiseguy, Man of Honor, Dress for Success.*

17. Picture of Sacred Heart of Jesus hanging over entrance to dining room, plastic mistletoe from last Christmas.

18. China closet that never got moved into the dining room because it was too heavy; contains espresso set, white porcelain with gold-leaf trim; espresso pot used five years ago to smuggle heroin; sugared almonds in plastic champagne glass (favor from cousin Danny's wedding).

19. Piano; nobody plays, but great trap for mlscellaneous loot.

Location, Location, Location

Where does a wiseguy

live? Anywhere he wants. Sure, he can afford a ritzy penthouse suite in Trump Tower or a sprawling estate on Long Island's North Shore, but if he's like most goodfellas, he'll gravitate toward familiar territory so he can hang with his homeboys. It may be an urban setting near the hustle and bustle of his social club, his pizzeria/money-laundering front, his goumada's travel agency. Or it could be a suburban spot, out of the eye of law enforcement officials— and of course, in a good school district for the kids. If he just can't make up his mind, here's a helpful little neighborhood profile:

If You're Thinking of Living In:

Bensonhurst

Bensonhurst is a colorful neighborhood steeped in tradition, with as many social clubs as there are streets. Located in lively west Brooklyn, Bensonhurst is ideally suited for the mobster on the move. The main thoroughfare, 18th Avenue, is a bustling commercial strip. At its intersection with 86th Street, "The Avenue," as it is known, is the hub of neighborhood activity, since some of Brooklyn's finest restau-

The 19th Hole: Below Par

rants and cafés are conveniently situated near an array of social clubs. (As an interesting aside, neighborhood folklore has it that there are more funeral parlors located per square foot in Bensonhurst than in any other part of the city.) Other key locations include twenty-four-hour diners, churches, and a high concentration of beauty parlors, bridal salons, video-rental stores, and card shops. Finally, the multitude of charming feasts ensures a permanent display of colored lights and other holiday finery.

If You're Thinking of Living in:

Howard Beach

Far from the hustle and bustle of the city, Howard Beach in south Queens is the quintessential all-American suburban enclave in a metropolitan area. Several prominent members of the community, including John Gotti, Vic Amuso, and Joe Massina, have chosen to make this place their home. Boasting one of the lowest crime rates in the city, Howard Beach is often described by some of its residents as "the safest f——n' neighborhood in the world!" Composed mostly of single-family dwellings, the streets of this locale provide a respite from the wiseguy's workaday world in more ways than one, with access to two major highways and key routes for trucks redirected from the adjacent John F.

Carmine Donofrio/New York Daily News photo

Gotti Residence: Keep Off Grass

Kennedy International Airport. Airport hotel lounges and lobbies provide convenient sites for important business meetings. Cross Bay Boulevard is the neighborhood's main thoroughfare, housing several popular gathering places.

Howard Beach is a model of middle-class values and, for its residents, a prime example of the symbolic move up and out of the "old neighborhood." But some traditions remain intact. Every Fourth of July in nearby Ozone Park, for example, John Gotti has hosted his famous barbecue and block party outside the Bergin Hunt and Fish Club. But for those who shun the crowds and yearn to blend in with their neighbors, Howard Beach offers the ultimate in pleasant anonymity.

If You're Thinking of Living In:

Massapequa

Once considered the holiday haven for the wealthy wiseguy, Massapequa on Long Island's south shore is now attracting the Family's younger generation. In years past several prominent Bosses have situated their summer homes in this beachfront community, but in recent years financially up-and-coming Mafia offspring looking for that idyllic suburban lifestyle have chosen the area for their primary residence. Sprawling manicured lawns provide ample room for their children at play, and her Jeep nestles cozily next to his Mercedes in the roomy two-car garage. Here leisure-time activities take on more prominence, as city social club scenarios yield to the family fun at the yacht club.

1. "Madonna in a bathtub" on lawn
2. Surveillance cameras around house
3. Satellite dish
4. American flag
5. NO numbers on house
6. Rottweiler or Doberman pinscher in yard
7. Christmas lights up all year long
8. Decals in door window that show donations to the PAL and Boy Scouts
9. "Beware of Owner!" sign on front gate
10. Sack of lime and extra garbage can in garage
11. Wreath made of yellow garbage bag twined with red, white, and blue ribbon, left over from Persian Gulf War

The Great Migration

Like so many families, the mob is always looking out for its kids. And as much as they want to see them get ahead, they don't exactly let them stray too far from home. Some Mafia offspring, however, have successfully made the break, getting as far away as New Jersey and central Long Island! (For some reason, they always take the southerly route.) Neighborhoods include Lodi and Fort Lee, both in New Jersey, and Long Island's Cedarhurst and Island Park.

Anthony "Gaspipe" Casso has been accused of doing away with the architect of his Mill Basin home. Who could blame him?

The Club Scene

When he's not at home or in jail, the wiseguy is at the center of his universe, the social club. Usually a nondescript storefront, and more than just a place to shoot the bull, the social club serves a multitude of mob functions:

As Business Headquarters

It's where the "button" comes in to get his marching orders from the skipper, who'll tell him what storeowner he has to "shake down" today, or in which parking lot he'll rendezvous with the union official who'll have the $5,000 cash kickback in a brown paper shopping bag.

It's also the site of the "sit-down," which involves those in the Family who have a "beef." The Boss usually presides over the "hearing"—which is more like a court-martial, with the firing squad to come later. He listens to both sides and tries to settle the dispute. If the mobster is guilty of the transgression, he'll be wise to own up to it right away and make amends; it helps in the life expectancy department.

As Discount House

The club is also a clearinghouse for all swag
(stolen goods) and a virtual shopping mall for all the
wiseguy's needs, whether it's a black leather jacket for
his goumada or a couple of cases of scotch for his
restaurant. The array of available goods can include—
literally—anything from soup to nuts. It usually works
like this: Each wiseguy has a list of what he can get his
hands on. Merchandise can include machine guns,
Treasury bonds, Ming vases, fifteenth–century art, or
twenty–five pounds of scallops. Word gets around to
the other clubs, and transactions are made like a sort
of swap meet. Everybody makes a profit.

As Gossip Central

What's a day at the club without a lit-
tle bitching and moaning? Wiseguys love talking
behind each other's backs. And the heads of the

Family are no exception. John Gotti claimed he loved Sammy The Bull, but privately he complained to Underboss Frank Locascio about Gravano's greed:

> GOTTI: It doesn't even bother me if he had six, seven companies, companies himself. You know what I would tell him? You would be, I'll tell him, 'Let me know when ya feel you're gonna choke. Keep that. [inaudible] you're gonna choke. But you're not doing that! You're creating a f——n' army inside an army.' You know what I'm saying, Frankie?

Sometimes, however, it's just a couple of guys sitting around talking about personal problems:

> LOCASCIO: Blue Cross? You covered under Blue Cross?
> GOTTI: Yeah.
> LOCASCIO: Extended coverage or something?
> GOTTI: Yeah, special kind of coverage, you know. God forbid [inaudible] nine years. But ah, but then fire insurance on the house, stupid things. Eh, forget about it! Couple a thousand a month, Frank.

Occasionally, despite all precautions, an interloper can infiltrate the sanctum sanctorum. The Mafia Handbook was able to get a peek inside the Bergin Hunt and Fish Club, a long-time hangout for the Gambino Crime Family. Here's what we found:

1. The standard poker-table in the center of the beige-walled room, green felt top, slots for the chips. A few broken-down wooden chairs and a couple of folding chairs.
2. A vinyl-covered couch against the right wall.
3. A bar in the rear. A few bottles of booze, a couple of empty glasses. On the wall behind the bar, two framed *Newsday* front pages showing a smiling John Gotti and the headline "Untouchable."
4. Near entrance, a VCR with the time blinking.
5. On left wall, 4´ x 3´ framed picture of boxing champ Rocky Marciano.
6. A framed black-and-white photo of Al Capone and his gang.
7. An orange sign with black letters that says "THIS PHONE IS BUGGED."
8. A couple of trophies (type unknown).
9. Framed collage of personal snapshots.
10. A small American flag.
11. A map of Italy.
12. A back door.

To ensure that nobody but wiseguys
enter the club's hallowed halls, the mob relies on
a variety of security measures:

1. **The Traditional System: The sixty- or
   seventy-year-old guy in a windbreaker
   who hangs around the front door.**

2. **The Hi-Tech: A German shepherd.**

3. **The Deluxe System: A Doberman
   pinscher.**

Social Clubs

At the time of this writing the social clubs listed here existed at the addresses indicated. Due to the nature of the business, however, locations may change at a moment's notice.

Manhattan

Victory Star
311 East 76th St.

Ravenite
247 Mulberry St.

Triangle
208 Sullivan St.

Hawaiian
Moonlighters Club
140 Mulberry St

A resourceful mob enthusiast poses as a handyman in an effort to gain entry to the "Members Only" Ravenite Social Club. He subsequently plunged two and a half feet to his death in circumstances that authorities later termed "peculiar."

Brooklyn

Veterans and Friends
1628 Bath Ave.

Veterans and Friends
1446 86th St.

Rayfield
7620 17th Ave.

Banner
7509 New Utrecht Ave.

Falcon
6815 Fort Hamilton
Pkwy.

Pompeii
6705 11th Ave.

Café on N
6336 Avenue N

Nestor
Between 235 and 237,
on 5th Ave.

Café Sicilia
6415 Bay Pkwy.

South Brooklyn
Athletic Club
2684 Coney Island
Ave.

Leonard Street Club
292 Leonard St.

Arlington
391 Manhattan Ave.

Carolyn's
461 Court St.

Seamens
469 Myrtle Ave.

Windsor
Community Club
1373 41st St.
Basement

Queens

Good Neighbors
106–06 101st Ave.
Ozone Park

Bergin Hunt and Fish
98–04 101st Ave.

Our Friends
97–52 99th St.
Ozone Park

Veterans
77–04 101st Ave.

The Trophy Club
64–28 Metropolitan
Ave.

Café Liberty
84–10 Liberty Ave.

69–54 Grand Ave.
Maspeth

Bronx

Giglio Boys Lodge
3205 Westchester
Ave.

Corleone Social Club
3205 Westchester
Ave.

Café Espresso
2339 Arthur Ave.

Café Romeo
625 Crescent Ave.

Arthur Ave.
between 2339
and 2343*

Staten Island

Verrazano Social Club
126 Fingerboard Rd.

96 Hancock St.

291 Sands Lane

* Another sign of the desire to be inconspicuous
is the deliberate use of confusing addresses.

Chapter Eight

Fun and Games

Fun and Games

For you and me, the ideal vacation provides the opportunity to get away from it all. That is, to leave behind the responsibilities and routines faced daily in the workplace. Not so for the wiseguy, for whom the perfect vacation entails indulging in more of "it all" (eating, gambling, hanging out with the guys) while enhancing his tan and, if time permits, taking the wife to see Jerry Vale.

The Simple Pleasures

Why bother with the suitcases and boarding passes when the pragmatic wiseguy can enjoy his free time closer to home? The mob neighborhood provides no lack of outlets for his preferred leisure-time activities. For example there's:

1) The track: The metropolitan area wiseguy is never far away from one. Options include Belmont Park, Aqueduct, Yonkers Raceway, and—assuming there's no rival family eagerly awaiting his next visit to Jersey—the Meadowlands. As a last resort, the wiseguy on a tight schedule can always utilize his lunch break to bet the ponies at his local neighborhood OTB.

2) Cards: *(continental, pinochle, poker, casino, briscola, scopa)*: There's always a card game in progress at the social club—and a shylock close by.

3) Casino games

(craps, barbut, baccarat, chemin de fer): The wiseguy who knows where to look can find one of these games going on every night of the week and amass a few thousand before the cops raid the joint and ruin a hard night's work.

4) Numbers:

An illegal version of lotto, the *number,* as it is commonly known, is determined by the last three digits of the day's betting handle at a predesignated area racetrack, and unwittingly published the following day in every newspaper's sports section.

5) Sports betting:

The wiseguy isn't going to be one of those people grilling barbecued chicken in the stadium parking lot before the Big Game. More than likely, he's the one taking action on the Giants, giving 6 ½ points to the Lions. However, like every other red-blooded American, the wiseguy views Superbowl Sunday as the culmination of the sporting year, and the day on which he gets rich off the vig, no matter who wins the game.

What the Average Joe Does on Superbowl Sunday

1. Buys a couple of kegs of beer.
2. Calls friends to invite them over for pregame beer blast.
3. Gathers friends around TV in living room just prior to kickoff.
4. Organizes $2.00 betting pool.
5. Mocks extravagance of half-time show.
6. Sends friends home with uneaten food.

What Joey "Numbers" Does on Superbowl Sunday

1. Buys the paper, checks for current betting line.
2. Calls other bookies to lay off action on extremely large bets (over $100,000).
3. Gathers friends around TV in social club just prior to kickoff.
4. Organizes $2,000 betting pool. Fixes outcome.
5. Bemoans lack of extravagance of half-time show.
6. Sends friends home with unmarked bills.

And there's always Atlantic City for a sublime mix of business and pleasure—including a quick hit at the gambling tables, or just a quick "hit."

Eating Right

Seasoned wiseguys are always on the lookout for three things: the company of other wiseguys, a good meal, and the Feds. Not coincidentally, several area restaurants frequently provide the setting for just such a confluence. (Hey, even the Feds like a good veal piccata every now and again.) If a wiseguy is at the next table, you know you're almost certain to have an excellent dinner.

Where They Eat and Greet

Manhattan

Rao's
455 E. 114th St.

Taormina's
147 Mulberry St.

Giambone's
42 Mulberry St.

Angelo's
146 Mulberry St.

Umberto's
129 Mulberry St.

Pulcinella's
1394 York Ave.

Manhattan Café
1161 1st Ave.

Brooklyn

Villa Vivolo
8829 26th Ave.

Tommaso's
1464 86th St.

Monte's Venetian Room
451 Carroll St.

Hotel Gregory
8315 4th Ave.

Gargiulo's
2911 W. 15th St.

Casa Rosa
384 Court St.

Queens

Parkside
107–01 Corona Ave.
Corona

Altadonna's
137–03 Cross Bay Blvd.
Ozone Park

Don Peppe's
135–58 Lefferts Blvd.
Ozone Park

Russo's on the Bay
162–45 Cross Bay Blvd.
Howard Beach

Villa Russo
118–16 101st Ave.
Richmond Hill

Café Giannini
66–12 Fresh Pond Rd.

Bronx

Amici's
566 E. 187th St.

Joe and Nina's
3019 Westchester Ave.

Staten Island

Ribs and More
1650 Hyland Blvd.

Plaza Pizza
60 New Dorp Plaza

Scarlett's
283 Sand Lane

Marina Café
154 Manson Ave.

Mangia! with the Mobsters

Joey Gallo ran more than just a social club on President Street in Brooklyn. He also had a swimming pool across the street for the kids in the neighborhood. In the summertime, he kept a little patio spot open for some dining al fresco, and he'd invite friends and acquaintances for a bite to eat. His cook, "Punchy," whipped up the following:

Pasta Joey Gallo (serves 4)

For Tomato Sauce
3 tablespoons olive oil
1 medium onion, chopped
1 teaspoon parsley, minced
1 clove garlic

1 large can Italian tomatoes
1 medium can tomato purée
½ teaspoon salt
½ teaspoon pepper
4 large leaves fresh basil or 1 teaspoon dried basil
1 teaspoon oregano
2 ½ cups freshly shelled green peas
1 pound "occhi di lupo" (wolf's eyes) pasta
grated Pecorino Romano or Parmesan cheese to taste

Sauté garlic and onion to golden color. Add can of tomatoes and simmer for fifteen minutes. Add tomato purée, shelled peas, and seasonings. Simmer for half an hour. Cook pasta until *al dente* (approximately 7 minutes) in boiling salted water. Drain pasta. Combine pasta with sauce; simmer. Serve with grated cheese to taste.

Tommaso Buscetta had plenty of time to

cook. The Sicilian Don who ratted out his counterparts in Sicily and the United States spent many long months in hiding under federal protection. He perfected not only his testimony but his recipes as well. As a man of impeccable taste and refinement, Buscetta settled only for the best ingredients—and he sent the federal agents out looking for them. Since he couldn't have any visitors, the agents benefited from Buscetta's feasts:

Penne Tommaso Buscetta (serves 4)

2 pounds ripe plum tomatoes
3 medium-sized cloves garlic
¾ cup fresh chopped basil
1 teaspoon oregano
⅔ cup virgin olive oil
1 pound penne
salt and pepper to taste

Blanch tomatoes and remove skins. Dice tomatoes and place them in a bowl. Coarsely chop garlic and combine with basil, oregano, and olive oil. Add to the bowl. Mix well, cover with aluminum foil, and marinate in refrigerator overnight. Cook penne until *al dente* (about 12 minutes) in large stockpot of boiling salted water. Drain quickly and combine with tomato mixture. Absolutely *do not* add grated cheese.

And Buscetta's *pasta di tutti pasti*:

Linguini and Clam Sauce (serves 4)

2 dozen littleneck clams

To clean clams
Scrub in cold water with stiff-bristled brush. Soak for three hours in cold brine of ⅓ cup salt to 1 gallon of cold water. Rinse under cold water.

To steam clams
Place clams in stockpot with water just covering bottom of pot. Put lid on pot, use medium flame, steam clams until opened (approximately 2 minutes). Remove clams and allow to cool. Remove clam meat and chop. Pass clam broth from pot through cheesecloth to remove any remaining sand. Save broth.

For sauce
⅓ cup virgin olive oil
2 large garlic cloves, minced
1 tablespoon chopped parsley
½ teaspoon salt
1 (28-ounce) can tomato purée
½ teaspoon crushed red pepper or black pepper (optional)

Lightly sauté garlic in olive oil. Add tomato purée and seasonings. Simmer for 20 minutes. Add clams and 1 cup of clam broth and simmer for 10 minutes. Boil 1 pound of linguini in salted water until *al dente*. Drain quickly; combine linguini and sauce.

Undercover cop Tommy Russo

knows what a good meal means to a mobster. He came up with the following recipe so that no one could doubt his assumed wiseguy identity. It's a fish dish that even the best social club chef would love.

Scampi à la Tommy Russo (serves 4)

2 tablespoons virgin olive oil
2 tablespoons melted butter
¼ cup lemon juice
pepper to taste
3 tablespoons shallots, finely minced
3 garlic cloves, finely minced
2 pounds jumbo shrimp, shelled and deveined

Combine olive oil, melted butter, lemon juice, pepper, shallots, and garlic in shallow baking dish. Add and turn several times to coat thoroughly. Place dish of shrimp in preheated broiler about 4 inches from heat for about 2 minutes. Turn and broil on the other side for about 1 minute. Arrange on platter and pour remaining sauce over shrimp. Garnish with lemon slices and sprinkle with parsley.

Family Fun

When business is slow and the wiseguy determines that the time is right to pack up the wife and kids for a little R & R, their destination is rarely in doubt. In this case, "goin' south" is taken literally, and almost invariably for the mob family on vacation, all roads lead to Florida. Why Florida? It's sunny, affordable, and, most important, it's where the wiseguys go!

To get his family to Florida, the wiseguy employs the services of an authorized travel agent, who must withstand scrutiny before being awarded one of those neat "Mob Approved" window decals.

Fort Lauderdale has long been one of the mob's favorite Florida vacation retreats. It's the place where Philadelphia crime boss Nicky Scarfo set up his elaborate waterfront vacation digs—the dining room was said to be so ornate that he had it cordoned off with velvet ropes. His backyard, however, was completely paved (except for one palm tree) in an apparent attempt to rid his property of any potential "bugging" devices. His boat, a thirty-eight-footer called "The Casablanca," bore the smaller subtitle "Usual

> **Q:** Hey, Don Martucci—you've just whacked your chief rival for control of the Jersey docks. What are you going to do now?
>
> **A:** I'm going to freakin' Disney World!

Suspects." John Gotti, before checking into his suite at the federal pen in Marion, Illinois, could occasionally be found guesting at the luxurious Harbor Beach Marriott. There's also Turnberry Isle—an exclusive condominium complex replete with marina, shops, and entertainment options constituting what one investigator calls a "mob resort."

Hanging Out

When he's in Fort Lauderdale, the wiseguy inevitably goes "bouncing" with his friends. He'll most likely turn up at Martha's on the Water, Joseph's, Frankie and Johnny's, Yesterday's, or, in Hollywood, Sonken's.

If he's shopping, he'll stop at Burdine's, Short's, or Belk-Lindsley for the finest in men's clothing. On occasion, a perfectly relaxing Florida vacation is interrupted by the clarion call of business. Maybe the Boss wants someone to check on the whereabouts of Johnny Sunshine, whom the Boss suspects is holed up somewhere in Florida with a quarter of a million dollars of missing Family money.

The boos of the Family is usually so

busy he has precious little time for vacation. That's why he'll try to arrange to set himself up with a luxurious weekend home, not far from his weekday residence. He'll have acres of land, raise horses, run a farm. There will be a swimming pool for summer use and snowmobiles for winter use. If he must go out of town for business, he'll take the goumada—and they'll turn it into a first-class trip. Las Vegas and Lake Tahoe are prime locations, where the Boss is usually comped. The red-carpet treatment includes the best suites, the best champagne, and the best seats in the house for the best shows (or Wayne Newton).

Prerequisites for a Mob Travel Agent

1. Must be goumada, relative, or friend.
2. Must have flexible hours.
3. Must have established working relationship with key customs officials at all major U.S. airports.
4. Must have shoddy record-keeping system frequently resulting in lost and shredded documents.
5. Must have thorough knowledge of all South American travel destinations, including indigenous climates, points of cultural and financial interest, and local extradition policies.

Traveling out of the country is avoided at all

costs because the wiseguy doesn't ever want to get "clocked" (have his movements monitored). Sometimes, though, he has little or no choice—for example, when he's jumping bail, escaping indictment, or entertaining an international business deal too lucrative to ignore.

Vacation Itinerary

Monday: Sit by pool, go to Calder racetrack with the boys, meet in-laws for early-bird dinner special.

Tuesday: Sit by pool, scout for new restaurant location, meet with Southern associates concerning impending "suicide" of mutual rival.

Wednesday: Sit by pool at goumada's heel, read the newspapers to her, check veracity of Johnny Sunshine sighting, go to Gulf Stream track with the boys, take wife to local dinner theater production of *Breaking Legs*.

Thursday: Sit by pool, hire a contractor to whack Johnny Sunshine, attend bingo marathon at Hallendale Jewish Seniors Center to establish alibi.

Friday: Go deep-sea fishing on friend's charter boat, drop off Johnny Sunshine, visit showroom back at marina, purchase small yacht with bingo winnings.

Saturday: Luau.

Sunday: Sit by pool, check out of hotel, destroy stolen credit cards, return rental car, turn back odometer (old habit), fly home.

Chapter Nine

Doing the Right Thing

Doing the Right Thing

Miss Mobster's Guide to Family Values

One of the sad casualties of the modern age is the beautiful code of manners handed down through the ages by La Cosa Nostra. Marvelously detailed and comprehensive, it provides guidance in all matters of life and death, from proper decorum to the proper technique for removing bloodstains. Its best defense against current charges of rigidity is that it provides an ideal of conduct in Family matters against which contemporary members are seen to fall terribly short. Whether this deterioration in behavior is merely a symptom or is, indeed, an active cause of the unhappy state of affairs prevailing in the Family today is a matter of dispute beyond the powers of Miss Mobster to resolve. However, a return to proper etiquette can only help to redress this unfortunate situation. Dire circumstances require extreme remedies, which is why it finally seems necessary, even advisable, to put the unwritten code into print. After all, family values are Family values.

The Christening

The beautiful ceremony of the christening is the Family's first opportunity to initiate a beloved infant into the fold. That it is an intimate occasion, suffused with the promise of new life, does not prevent its being governed by a strict set of rules.

Selection of the Godfather

The single most important decision necessitated by this ceremony is the choice of Godfather, a role whose importance is as much symbolic as practical. Generally a figure of some stature in the community, the Godfather should be a

Family member who can provide spiritual and material guidance for the child as he matures.

Invitations

To prevent unwanted guests (including lower-level law-enforcement officials equipped with surveillance equipment) from attending the ceremony, it is wise to follow the charming custom of delivering invitations by hand rather than entrusting them to the U.S. Postal System.

Attire

It is customary for the infant, regardless of sex, to wear a full-length white-lace christening gown. Although in a more gracious age this was lovingly stitched by the child's grandmother, it is, regrettably, more and more common to purchase it off the rack.

The adults attending are expected to wear sober attire suitable for church-going. For men, dark suits and white shirts are appropriate. For women, demure dresses with no decolletage or a simple skirt and jacket ensemble are acceptable.

Guest List

Attendance should be strictly limited to Family members.

Compensation for Clergy

A few hundred dollars discreetly slipped to the priest officiating at the ceremony may be seen as an investment in *his* discretion as well as an encouragement of his loyalty at some future time, should he be required to turn a blind eye to a misdemeanor committed by Junior when he reaches a riper age. It may even help Junior get to heaven faster.

Gifts

The christening is an initiation in more ways than one since it is on this solemn occasion that the future Family member (God willing) receives the first in a long line of envelopes filled with money. It hardly seems necessary to stress that such presents be given in the form of bills rather than checks (so dangerous) or traveler's checks (so vulgar). In this sad time of ignorance, however, it may also be necessary to mention that no name should go on the envelope and no card should be enclosed. Rest assured that the child's parents will know from whom the gift was received.

It is difficult to pinpoint the proper amount to give since it varies with geographical area, inflation, and one's closeness to the parents and child in question. However, a good rule in all Family matters is, when in doubt, be generous. This is a rule that one may not live to regret. Consider it an investment not only in the child's future, but in your own.

Dear Miss Mobster:

Q: *Is it appropriate to make a donation to the church in the child's name?*

A: *Yes, as long as it's in his first name only.*

Dear Miss Mobster:

Q: *Am I supposed to kiss the Godfather's ring?*

A: *Not unless you want to look like a big jerk.*

The Wedding

A truly joyous event, the wedding is an elaborate display of love and friendship. It's also a contest to determine who can put on the ritziest reception by spending the least amount of money. Of course, the liquor, flowers, bridesmaids' dresses, etc., all come through "connections"— even the catering hall is probably run by someone in the Family. The wedding is a significant rite of passage, marking the official beginning of a new relationship—that of the wiseguy with his goumada.

Invitations
See *The Christening*.

Attire
One finds a changing trend in this department. Since the majority of guests at Family functions attend many more funerals than weddings, black seems to be the color of choice for both men and women. The bride, of course, wears traditional white with the very large veil required to cover hair that has achieved unprecedented altitude on her very special day.

The Receiving Line
A first-time guest may question why there is more than one receiving line at the reception. One line, of course, heads

toward the bride and groom, who receive everyone's best wishes.

The second line is directed to the father of the bride, who collects the gifts. This must be done personally because gifts are, of course, unmarked. Since the gifts are in the form of cash, they have to be handled very carefully, so the father is normally attended by one of his closest friends. The friend is actually an armed guard for A BUSTA—the little bag into which the envelopes are deposited and which is later carried by the bride.

The third line is designated for the Boss, who remains seated to receive his tribute of respect.

Seating Arrangements

The standard rule at all weddings is that Families sit together. Tables are made up of a group of "business" associates, not unlike the seating arrangement at a corporate convention or the annual softball league awards banquet. As in those functions, men are invited without their wives, a practice allied with the venerable tradition of the 10:00 p.m. Exodus, tacitly understood to be the hour when most goodfellas depart to spend their Saturday nights in the company of their goumadas.

Entertainment

It should be the best money can buy. A lounge singer, a rock band for the young people, a "big band" for the older crowd, or, if circumstances allow, a name act. But there is rarely any dancing because men tend to outnumber women by a ratio of 20 to 1. They're generally discussing business in any case, and it is certainly frowned upon for them to dance with one another, even in these dissolute times.

Dear Miss Mobster:

Q: Do I give my tribute of respect to the happy couple in singles or in twenties?

A: The denominations are up to your discretion as long as they add up to $10,000.

Dear Miss Mobster:

Q: Is it acceptable to wear my white spandex micro-mini to the wedding?

A: Not unless you want the bridesmaids to beat you to a pulp and dump you in the last stall of the ladies' room.

Introductions

Proper forms of acknowledgment, greeting, and salutation are crucial tools in the wiseguy's business and social trade. The introduction is extremely important; its form varies with the purpose.

Basic Introduction
Mobster A (any rank) summons Mobster B to introduce him to an associate, C:

"Hey [or "Yo"] Bobby, this is Billy 'Bats.' He's a—*friend of mine.*" They give each other the once-over as they shake hands. The appellation "friend of mine" connotes that associate C is not a made member of the family—but has potential.

Informal Introduction
Arm extended, Mobster A summons Mobster B to introduce person C, who is not necessarily in the Family but may be useful to know:

"Hey [or "Yo"] Bobby, this is Jerry." They shake hands.

Formal Introduction
Mobster A (any rank) summons Mobster B to introduce him to Mobster C:

"Hey [or "Yo"] Bobby, how ya doin'? This is Vinny 'Botts,'

a friend of ours." All three shake hands, and check one another out as they kiss on the cheek. The distinction "friend of ours" means he is a made member of a Family and can turn out to be either a good friend or a worst enemy.

Very Formal Introduction

Capo A summons Mobster B to meet the Boss. Capo A says, "John, this is Nicky." The two shake hands.

Mobster B must appear humble and make some appropriately flattering remark, such as, "It is an honor" or "I am full of respect." He should *not* say, "Nice suit." Kissing the ring and genuflecting are considered outmoded forms of admiration, having been replaced by the custom of giving considerable cash contributions to the Family. It is important to note that in the Very Formal Introduction, nicknames are not used. The Boss need not say anything. He is required only to incline his head in acknowledgment—and to keep a steely gaze on Nicky to unnerve him for the rest of the night.

If a wiseguy doesn't recognize a face at a function, it is perfectly appropriate for him to approach the Unknown Person. The correct form of address is "Who you wit'?" This serves the purpose of discovering a) if the Unknown Person is or isn't a made man, and b) whom he knows. If he's a made man, he simply gives his nickname or his capo's name. An associate, however, must explain, "I'm with Joey Shoes." It's up to Joey Shoes to come to his friend's rescue, explaining, "He's with me," or "He's with us," thus vouching for someone who is not a member of the Family.

The Wake

Although it may be a regrettable occasion, the wake is one of the most eagerly anticipated functions requiring a wiseguy's attendance. Aside from his joy at not being the object of the mortician's attentions, the wiseguy welcomes the opportunity to socialize on a grand scale.

Wakes are, in fact, regarded as "Little Appalachins" because they are the local versions of what amounted to a national mob "convention" at an upstate New York farm back in 1957.

It is important to note who *doesn't* show up at the viewing: Those conspicuous by their absence are probably the ones who contracted the "piece of work." Wakes are typically well-attended: A large percentage of mourners never knew the deceased but are looking to get made. The astute wannabe will seize the opportunity to attend since he now knows that the Family is down a member and the books will "open up." As when searching for that rare Manhattan apartment, the first thing to do is scan the obituaries in the local newspaper.

Lawyers also make their presence felt, not only to pay their respects to the deceased but to attract potential clients as well. In this capacity, they are often referred to as "hearse chasers."

Proper Decorum

There are certain rules of behavior for those saying goodbye to the goodfella.

Wives and ex-wives: Usually relegated to opposite sides of the room, where they can each greet the long line of guests separately. Boxes of tissues are in ample supply. A relative or friend is on hand keeping track of hundreds of anonymous floral displays that fill the room.

Boss: His ceremonial function requires a tasteful display of condolence and respect to the immediate family of the deceased. His presence is required to conduct Family affairs.

Made members: They pay respects to the immediate family, and then pay respects to the Boss.

Wannabes: They are careful to follow the lead of made mentors, then they retire to the back of the room or the lounge to remain on the scene without getting in anyone's way.

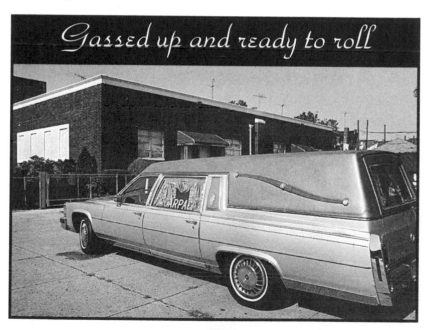

Gassed up and ready to roll

Goumada: Her appearance is made either before or after regular viewing hours. The friends of the deceased work out the arrangements so she can pay her final respects and confirm that her erstwhile boyfriend is really dead.

Funerals

In order to appreciate the stateliness and dignity of a Mafia funeral, it is necessary to liken it to a military burial with full honors. After all, most of the deceaseds did die in the line of duty. (For proper behavior, consult the section on wakes.) The mob funeral provides special challenges for officiating clergy, who generally restrict the eulogy to generalities and often resort, in closing, to the rather noncommittal statement "And only God makes the Final Judgment."

The funeral is always held in the wiseguy's "old neighborhood," the place that witnessed his boyhood joys, sorrows, and peccadilloes. It is customary for the entire population of the neighborhood to attend, although most attendees have not been in church since the unfortunate wiseguy got married.

Miss Mobster's Requirements for a Criminally Correct Mob Funeral Procession

1.   50 limousines.
2.   10 flower cars.
3.   500 pairs of sunglasses: for the grieving family and for the wiseguys who don't want their faces showing up in the latest round of surveillance photos.
4.   The most expensive casket there is. Even in death, a wiseguy must keep up appearances.
5.   10 pallbearers—in case the funeral director was "urged" to hide another body inside.
6.   Directly behind the casket, the immediate family.
7.   Behind them, the Family.
8.   Behind them, selected representatives from other Families.
9.   Bringing up the rear, a flock of hopefuls.
10. At the church, the same group of old ladies who go to every wedding and funeral.
11. Outside the church, the rest of the neighborhood, some of whom wipe a tear from their eyes, others of whom try to wipe the smirk off their faces.

Dear Miss Mobster:

Q: Is *it appropriate to take a holy card when leaving a wake?*

A: It is not only appropriate, it is de rigueur, especially if your attendance has had the hoped-for result. Just be sure to avoid the laminated cards—the smell of the burning plastic is so unpleasant.

Dear Miss Mobster:

Q: May I make a play for the widow?

A: Go ahead. It's your funeral.

Dear Miss Mobster:

Q: What kind of sunglasses constitute appropriate funeral wear?

A: The bullet-proof kind.

Epilogue

The Future of
the Mob

by Claire Sterling

Judging from the record over the past two thousand years, there will always be a mob.

The Mafia, pronounced dead many times over, has outlived a Jewish mob, an Irish mob, and every other mob in American history. If it is supposedly sliding into irreversible decline at last—another premature pronouncement—several others can hardly wait to take its place.

The Yakuza is the latest offspring of the Bakuto gambling gangs working Japan's medieval highways in the 1600s.

The Russian mafia descends from a Thieves' World that formed up to fight the Tsar in the 1850s.

The Chinese Triads replaced an Origin of Chaos Society, replacing a long line of predecessors from the Yellow Turbans to the White Lotus Society, to the Copper Horses and Iron Shins, to the Red Eyebrows in the year A.D. 90.

As for the original Mafia model in Sicily, emerging nearly one hundred and fifty years ago, it replaced a succession of earlier models going back to the Sicilian Vespers uprising five hundred years before that.

These are the patricians of the international underworld, the oldest, largest, wealthiest, and most sophisticated crime syndicates operating around the globe—the supreme survivors.

But they are no longer a privileged few. America, Europe, Asia, Africa, and the Orient are infested with proliferating criminal bands: from the Colombian cocaine cartels and Turkish arms-drugs mafia to a profusion of Yugoslavs, Poles, Puerto Ricans, Mexicans, Nigerians, Ghanaians, Rumanians, Albanians, Pakistanis, Sri Lankans, Vietnamese, Koreans, Philippinos, Jamaicans, Colombians, Moroccans (not to mention Bloods and Crips, Hell's Angels, and so on).

Practically everybody in the crime business today is organized, which goes far to explain why lawful societies are losing the war on the underworld: Their guns are pointing in the wrong direction.

There are no laws against organized crime in nearly all the countries afflicted by it. The United States, a pioneer in the field, sends felons to jail for "continuing criminal conspiracy." Italy does the same for "association with the Mafia," putting a man behind bars for up to six years. They are the only ones.

Almost universally, the entire structure of law enforcement—legislation, courts, police—is directed against the individual criminal, a vanishing species. So, while its foot soldiers are picked off one by one, the enemy continues to advance, as it has advanced relentlessly for a quarter of a century.

Obviously it is safer to be an organized criminal than a loner. Yet safety isn't all. Nor is the supposedly supreme reward—making money without working for it—always as rewarding as it looks. Wiseguys often suffer from acid stomach, ulcers, high blood pressure, heart trouble, and all-around stress: too much hard work. The mortality rate is high as well.

Clearly there is something else about collective delinquency that gives it powerful age-old appeal. Joining up is not just a matter of beating the law, but of sharing secrets, indulging in mystic rituals, inventing in-house rules, playing the tough guy, feeling superior to ordinary suckers, and belonging to an exclusive club.

Criminal brotherhoods separated by thousands of miles and centuries of history are remarkably similar in such matters.

The Sicilian Mafia and Chinese Triads, a continent apart, use similar blood oaths to frighten a member into silence and obedience for life. The Mafia candidate holds in his hand a burning saint's image stained with his blood and swears his fealty; the Triad holds a burning yellow paper, mixes the ash with chicken blood, and drinks it.

Russian mafiosi and Japanese Yakuza cover their bodies with excruciatingly painful tattoos to prove their manliness.

All the patrician brotherhoods named above have elaborate in-house rules studded with death penalties: for collaborating with the law; for lying to, stealing from, or sleeping with the wife of a fellow member; or for trespassing on another member's turf.

Many such customs are falling away, swept aside by the liberating force of modern criminal pursuits. But liberation has opened horizons beyond imagining for organized crime.

Today's world has no frontiers for the mob, wherever it is. The American and Sicilian Mafias are crossing over freely into Eastern Europe and Russia. The Russian mafia is invading Western Europe and America. The Triads and Yakuza have been doing as much for years. Myriad gangs of hoods are hiring out to the larger ones, subalterns in turn to the big transcontinental players.

There are unbelievable profits to be made on the planetary circuit: half a trillion dollars a year in drugs alone, enough for them all. None of the big syndicates are going to war over the take. They have divided the territory worldwide: so we are told by defectors from their highest echelons.

Does the mob have a future in this day and age? Sure it does.

Claire Sterling, the author most recently of *Octopus: The Long Reach of the International Sicilian Mafia,* is a well–known expert on organized crime

GLOSSARY

administration: the upper-level power structure of an organized crime Family, composed of the boss, under-boss, and consiglieri.

a busta: the Mafia bride's white drawstring bag that's too small to hold all the cash gifts she receives at the wedding reception; also a general term for money.

associate: an almost-there; someone who works with and for wiseguys, but who hasn't been sworn in as a member of the Family.

beef: a complaint or disagreement within the organization, usually discussed during a sit-down with higher-ups in the Family.

books, the: euphemism for membership in the Family, since nothing is ever written down. When there is an availability (when someone dies), the books are "opened." When no one is being "made," the books are "closed."

borgata: a crime Family; brugad.

boss: the head of the crime Family; he is the only one who gives permission to "whack" or "make" someone, and he makes money from all Family operations; syns., don, chairman.

broken: demoted in rank; "knocked down."

brugad: a crime family; borgata.

burn: to murder; syns., break an egg, clip, do a piece of work, hit, ice, put out a contract on, whack.

button: a "made" member of the Mafia; soldier, wiseguy, goodfella, Man of Honor.

cafone: a phony or embarrassment to himself and others; "gavone" (slang pronunciation)

capo: ranking member of a Family who heads a crew (or group) of soldiers; a skipper, short for "capodecina."

chased: to be banished from the Mafia and barred from associating or doing business with any made members. The punishment is merciful in that the offender is spared death.

cleaning: taking the necessary steps (driving around, stopping in various locations) to avoid being followed.

clip: to murder; *see* burn.

clock: to keep track of someone's movements and activities.

comare: a Mafia mistress; "goumada" (slang pronunciation).

consiglieri: the counselor in a crime Family; advises boss and handles disputes within the ranks.

crew: a group of soldiers that takes orders from a capo.

cugine: a young toughguy looking to be made.

do a piece of work: to murder; *see* burn.

earner: someone whose expertise is making money for the Family.

empty suit: someone with nothing to offer who tries to hang around with mobsters.

enforcer: a person who threatens, maims, or kills someone who doesn't cooperate with Family rules or deals.

fence: someone with worldwide outlets to liquidate swag.

friend of mine: introduction of a third person who is not a member of the Family but who can be vouched for by a Family member.

friend of ours: introduction of one made member to another.

gavone: see cafone.

going south: stealing, passing money under the table, going on the lam.

goumada: see comare.

hard-on with a suitcase: mob lawyer; *fem.* half a hard-on with a suitcase.

hot place: a location suspected of being the target of law enforcement surveillance.

ice: to murder; *see* burn.

joint, the: where he goes when he slips up; *syns.,* the can, the pen.

loan shark: someone who lends mob money at an exorbitant interest rate; a shylock.

made: to be sworn into La Cosa Nostra: *syns.,* to be "straightened out," to get your button.

make a marriage: to bring two parties together for legitimate or illegitimate Family issues.

meat eater: a corrupt cop (not exclusively mobspeak).

nut, the: mobspeak for "the bottom line"; also the gross profit figure.

Omertå: the code of silence and one of the premier vows taken when being sworn into the Family. Violation is punishable by death.

off the record: an action taken without the knowledge or approval of the Family.

on the record: an action sanctioned by the Family.

piece: a gun.

pinched: arrested.

rat: a member who violates Omertá; *syns.,* squealer,

canary, snitch, stool pigeon.

sit-down: a meeting with the Family administration to settle disputes.

skipper: a capo.

swag: stolen goods.

vig: the interest payment on a loan from a loanshark (short for "vigorish").

vouch for: to personally guarantee—with one's life—the reputation of someone dealing with the Family.

walk and talk: a mobile discussion on sensitive matters undertaken to avoid listening devices.

whack: to murder; *see* burn.

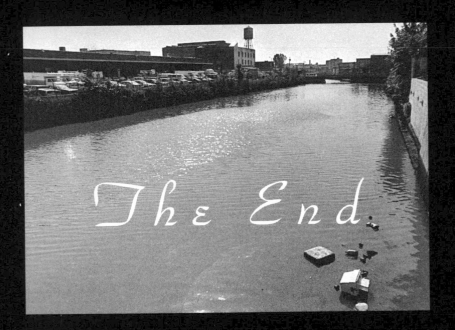

The End.